WHY ALCOHOLICS ANONYMOUS WORKS

by

Hal Bee

Hal Bee can be reached at

halbee124u@gmail.com

Copyright © 2020 Hal Bee

All rights reserved.

ISBN: **13-979-8-653-00139-0**

Table of Contents

Preface vii

Logically Speaking 1

Observations, Not Opinions 13

Disease And The Law 32

Two Histories 44

A Legal Background 66

The Paradoxical Power Of Faith 82

The Real Deal Of Righteousness 98

Making The Invisible Visible 107

The Puzzle of Pride 116

Life Under The Law 130

Taking Right Steps In The Wrong Direction 144

AA Alone 152

The Greatest Genus Of Alcoholics Anonymous 170

A Charming Couple 178

It Works, It Really Does 189

Conclusion 199

Appendix 203

Dedicated with much love and appreciation to:

William C. Swinney who provided inspiration when I needed it most

Julia H. who believed alone

Greg B. who is an instrument of God

And my hero, Bob McKinney who is the kindest man I've ever met.

Why Alcoholics Anonymous Works

Preface

The book *Alcoholics Anonymous* brilliantly describes "how" Alcoholics Anonymous (AA) works. "Why" Alcoholics Anonymous works has been obscured by misunderstanding and paradox since the fellowship's founding in 1935. The "why" has become even more mysterious as the fellowship has grown.

Understanding the "why" of AA is not necessary to get sober. This book is not important to AA newcomers. In fact, it is not recommended for those trying to get sober. The first 164 pages of the book *Alcoholics Anonymous* requires no elaboration. If you're an AA newcomer get a sponsor and take the Steps. Put this book on the shelf for later. Read it to celebrate your third AA birthday.

On the other hand, understanding the "why" of AA can be of great benefit for those who have been around the program for several years. Also, understanding the "why" will hopefully be of tremendous aid to those who enjoyed long-term sobriety and relapsed. It is no secret those who "pull the trigger" and drink again after many years in the AA program have a hard time regaining their sober footing. This book should be of tremendous value to these fellow trudgers. Helping those who have relapsed after a long period of sobriety motivates the author.

Christians mystified by AA's success sobering hopeless alcoholics will get an explanation they do not expect. AA is not a cult or massive group therapy. Should a Christian be in disagreement with the logic used in this book, an alternative explanation of AA sobriety is a requirement to maintaining your intellectual honesty. The precepts of this book rest on AA's incredible success over the last 85 years.

Chapter One
Logically Speaking

The secret to life is gratitude. No matter how bad things get, no matter how great the emotional pain, if an indelible gratitude colors the soul, peace prevails. Peace in the midst of the most horrid suffering is possible for those who are blessed with gratitude's irrepressible humility. Thankfulness for God's providence, given by God, transforms the soul and creates a new, untouchable "joy place" in the human heart. Thusly-gifted hearts may experience the deepest sorrow but never the despair of emptiness.

The human heart ensconced in an indelible gratitude is a mysterious thing. The blessing of this wondrous, deep and enduring gratitude is born in the unseen world where God rules openly then comes to earthly hearts and minds where God doesn't rule openly.[1] This holy gratitude, this evidence of God, this evidence of the unseen, this mysterious kept-promise of Scripture, is the ultimate human experience. Nothing counter weighs the misery wreaked by the rebellious human nature and this fallen world so effectively as does holy gratitude.

For an immortal human soul, hosted for only a blink of eternity's eye in a fragile, mortal body, the promise of everlasting life in heaven is the almost-perfect assurance, the producer of the almost-perfect gratitude. In

---

[1] Jesus taught us to pray that God's will would be done on earth as it is in heaven. Matthew 6:9

this one respect all religions of mankind offer a generic, indistinguishable assurance that produces an almost-perfect gratitude. There is but one exception.

Biblical Christianity's belief system stands in stark contrast to every other theology of man when it comes to producing gratitude. Biblical Christianity perfects the almost-perfect gratitude of other belief systems' promises. To produce the perfect gratitude heaven and a peaceful thought-life must be a gift. The promise of eternal life in heavenly nirvana to those who do not deserve it, nor must earn it, is Christianity's atomic distinction. The Gospel's promise to the undeserving bellows the hottest fires of gratitude in the human thought-life, both conscience and sub conscience. That's logic, not Christian-biased hyperbole'.

The Gospel only makes promises to those who admit they don't deserve it and can't earn it. Christians believe they are judged by God based on the morality of Jesus. They believe Jesus "imputed righteousness" is righteousness for them. The requirements of God's law are fulfilled in this way for the Christian. Right Christian doctrine denies any *quid pro quo* arrangement with God.

Earning heaven, or God's love, to whatever extent, diminishes gratitude. Any reasonable person would concede gratitude for receiving something that is "given" is greater than gratitude for receiving something that is "earned" or "deserved." If gratitude is the secret to life then the Gospel is a "must read" even for the most die-hard secularist.

A practicing alcoholic or substance abuser realizes a spiritual death in life. Lack of true gratitude is the trademark of addiction in humans. Those addicted to substances who experience God's grace and mercy in being delivered from the compulsion to imbibe, find more than a new hope. A protective gratitude comes with such a deliverance.

The gift of sobriety found in Alcoholics Anonymous (AA) is marked by an understanding the gift is neither deserved nor sufficiently earned. Not understanding sobriety is a gift bars the addiction's removal in the addicted. This is a spiritual law without exception. In AA the tornado lives led by alcoholics allow the recovered alcoholic to acknowledge this Devine gift as unmerited with unique ease. The alcoholic's hopeless dilemma plied with the antidote of a spiritual experience gins a mighty gratitude. When hopelessness is supplanted with hope, the result is a thankfulness very, very high up the gratitude meter. Though not eternal life, it is new life given to those walking on this side of the grass. The spiritual deliverance realized in Alcoholics Anonymous produces "must read" material too.

If both the Church and Alcoholics Anonymous claim members who thrive on unmerited gratitude, it is no leap of logic to suppose AA is somehow intertwined with the Gospel. It certainly has to pique the curiosity of those interested in investigating a power that comes from unseen places with the force to radically change lives. The shared foundation of "gratitude" between Alcoholics Anonymous and Christianity is an inseparable bond.

    The Bible is replete with descriptions of believers as being the "chosen." Any claim of being chosen by God, as is the case with those who subscribe to a branch of Christianity known as Reformed theology, infers there are those not chosen by God. The Reformed Christians' claim, on its face, appears to be the epitome of arrogance. One might surmise those individuals considering themselves "chosen" by God to the exclusion of others lack humility, extremely. Paradoxically, just the opposite is true.

    Being chosen by God leaves no room for one to take credit for personal salvation. The Scriptures are clear. God shares His glory with no one. The first Commandant[2] leaves no room for the Bible believer to argue that point.

    Those who believe in Reformed theology accept, or try to accept, their faith in Christ is the result of blind luck. They consider themselves fortunate God's plan to bring Himself glory has them playing the role of Christian. It is purely by God's grace and mercy the Reformed Christian comes to a liberating faith in Christ. They have nothing to brag about as Ephesians 2:8-9 reminds us. *For it is by grace you have been saved,*

---

[2] The first of the Ten Commandments is "I am the Lord thy God, thou shalt have no other Gods before me."

through faith-and this is not of yourselves, it is the gift of God- not by works, so that no one can boast. That's unavoidable humility. No grace is nudged out. No gratitude for salvation is watered down.

Reformed Christians also believe God's grace is "irresistible grace." Like the alcoholic who tries every means to carry on until forced to surrender, the Reformed believe "the chosen" are pursued by God before surrendering to their "election." The doctrine of "irresistible grace" is the coup de gras for any of the "elected" tempted to steal God's glory by taking a smidgen of credit for their faith.

The AA experience confirms this truth of Scripture as construed by Reformed Christians. According to the book *Alcoholics Anonymous*, the program of AA is not available to those who are *"constitutionally incapable of being honest with themselves."*[3] The AA text goes on to say, *"They are not at fault. They seem to have been born that way."*[4] The Reformed doctrine of election and the contention believers are "chosen" could not be more functionally represented than it is in AA.

The counterfactual belief system to Reformed theology's "irresistible grace" is a branch of Christianity called Arminianism. Arminians, predisposed to legalism, believe the Christian must choose God in response to His

---

[3] *Alcoholics Anonymous*, (New York: Alcoholics Anonymous World Services, Inc., 2001, Forth Edition), p 58

[4] Ibid

prompting. The Arminian doctrine concludes God gave us free will to decide to "pray the prayer," or not. The Armenian perspective cannot avoid giving the saved some credit, however minute, for their salvation. The Armenian shares God's glory. At the end of the day, their only available evangelistic homily is, "pick God and be smart like me." That is unavoidable arrogance, to whatever degree, and it minimizes gratitude for God's grace. Again, that's pure logic.

  The paradoxical truth regarding humility is exposed by the Reformed versus Armenian debate. That God discloses himself to the Armenian Christian as He does is none of the author's business. After much research, much trial and error, the author has determined conclusively he is not the Holy Spirit.

  When pointing out Christians who eat meat sacrificed to idols are more mature spiritually than those that don't, (note the legalist is spiritually immature), the Apostle Paul confirms Christian opinions can be different and right simultaneously. The author <u>does not</u> assert Arminian believers are not Christians bound for heaven. The author <u>does</u> assert Arminianism is, for reasons herein explained, not aligned with the principles outlined in the 12 Steps of Alcoholics Anonymous. Addressing addiction has proven to require every scrap of gratitude and humility that can be scrounged.

  The Armenian would ask why God gave believers the Great Commission to go out and make disciples if the determination has already been made. It's a legitimate question. Alcoholics Anonymous fulfills the Great Commission in a way that fully answers the Armenian question and in a way Reformed Christians don't recognize. The Reformed would do well to thoroughly understand AA's philosophy. The rooms of Alcoholics Anonymous are an exaggerated illustration of how the Great Commission benefits both parties in the evangelistic equation. A witness to the Gospel comes away edified even if the would-be disciple remains unmoved. AA was founded on the truth no activity immunes the alcoholic from alcohol like witnessing (sharing their experience, not preaching) to another alcoholic. The AA fellowship's proliferation, longevity and success is the Great Commission at work in a very special way, as we shall see.

Alcoholics Anonymous is a fellowship of men and women who take their name from the book of the same title published in 1939. The longest tenure of sobriety at this time was barely four years. The fellowship's name has been coined into the shortened moniker of "AA," which is known worldwide.

Ask an AA member why they recovered from addiction to alcohol when so many don't and to a person they plead bafflement. Outside some design of the Almighty there is no explanation why they survive while so many others perish. These survivors are no smarter than those who perish nor have they suffered more, or less. The only intellectually honest conclusion can be that God did for them what they could not do for themselves.[5]

These "Reformed" drinkers (pun intended) are able to take certain steps suggested by the book *Alcoholics Anonymous* and a "spiritual awakening" happens. As my AA friend Louis loves to say, "take those first nine steps and God is going to show up, like it or not." Some alcoholics wanting to recover have the honesty to take the Steps of AA, some don't.

The text *Alcoholics Anonymous* is fondly referred to in the fellowship as the "Big Book." The Bible is referred to as "The Great Big Book." The first 164 pages of the Big Book are the textbook of recovery from substance abuse, the last 411 pages are testimonials and appendices. I have found no error in this textbook nor any promise made therein unkept. Surprisingly to some, I have found nothing in contradiction to a Reformed theologian's reading of the Bible.

Why Alcoholics Anonymous Works shows AA success comes from the cohesion of thought and practice found between Reformed theology and the methodology outlined in the book *Alcoholics Anonymous*. The correlation and symmetry is not what most churchgoers or recovered alcoholics think. Upon close inspection, the sober alcoholics of AA strangely, serendipitously, testify to the deity of Christ.

---

[5] Ibid., p. 84

God uses the fellowship of AA to bring about sobriety using Biblical concepts as described in the first 164 pages of the book. The most prominent tool used in describing and exemplifying these paradoxical concepts is the 12 Steps of recovery. This book is not an enervate introspection of the 12 Steps but the Steps are discussed and analyzed.

For future reference here are the famous 12 Steps of recovery as found on page 59 of the book *Alcoholics Anonymous*:

1. Admitted we were powerless over alcohol and that our lives were unmanageable.
2. Came to believe that a power greater than ourselves could restore us to sanity.
3. Made a decision to turn our will and our lives over to the care of God as we understand him.
4. Made a searching and fearless moral inventory of ourselves.
5. Admitted to God, to ourselves and another person the exact nature of our wrongs.
6. Were entirely ready to have God remove these defects of character.
7. Humbly ask Him to remove our shortcomings.
8. Made a list of persons we had harmed and became willing to make amends to them all.
9. Made direct amends to those we had harmed except when to do so would injure them or others.

10. Continued to take personal inventory and when we were wrong promptly admit it.
11. Sought through prayer and mediation to improve our conscience contact with God praying only for knowledge of His will for us and the power to carry it out.
12. Having had a spiritual awakening as the result of these steps we tried to carry this message to alcoholics and practice these principles in all our affairs.

These 12 Steps have led to the formation of Narcotics Anonymous, Overeaters Anonymous, and many like groups. For those addicted to other substances, or who have loved ones so addicted, you will not be cheated by substituting "addiction" for "alcoholism" or "drugs" for "alcohol" in these pages. On the contrary, what is explained herein particularly addresses any distinctions to show they are meaningless.

The author has few typical credentials. He has read the book *Alcoholics Anonymous* many times and no two of those journeys were the same. Reading descriptions of paradox and exploring examples of paradox are like that.

The author has experienced a spiritual awakening as the result of taking the 12 Steps as described in Step 12. He has been blessed with a psychic change as promised by the book *Alcoholics Anonymous*.[6] He has experienced the paradoxical freedom that comes with

---

[6] Ibid., The Doctor's Opinion, XXV

surrender. He has experienced the power found in a powerlessness soaked in grace. On his good days he finds freedom from the bondage of "self."

The author has also explored the tenants of Reformed theology and made several readings of the Bible. No two of those journeys were the same either. Reading descriptions of paradox and exploring examples of paradox are like that.

The author has experienced the forgiveness and freedom that comes with believing Jesus is exactly who he claims to be. In church words, to gain "street cred" with the Christian doctrinal purist- the author recites the Apostle's Creed in full belief. On good days he carries the reality of Jesus in the front of his mind. On bad days he doesn't. He likes the freedom of forgiving and being forgiven on good days too.

The challenge of writing this book is the distinctiveness of its two intended audiences, recovered alcoholics and Christians, Reformed Christians in particular. Let me apologize upfront to the recovered alcoholics. The Gospel offended me the first time I heard it too. My reaction to being shown the Bible propounds that deep down people are not good made me recoil as well. Please do not be discouraged and keep the open mind you will need. Ruffled feathers at first hearing should, by now, send up the spiritual antenna of AA trudgers. Also, recovered alcoholics will recognize much of what is written in some of the chapters. The Christians

Logically Speaking

have to be brought up to speed on AA doctrine and context for you is important. Please bear with me. These pages illuminate a new path to much love and freedom for those who persevere to the end. I promise.

To the Christian I also promise an open mind will be rewarded. Herein the truth of Scripture is sustained not denied. There is much to be learned by understanding the Biblical principles of Alcoholics Anonymous and examining the AA experience without prejudice. The open-minded churchgoer will see evidence that God is moving in AA and maybe even gain guiltless permission to admire and encourage His AA handiwork.

Both AA and the church can be strengthened by affirmation and loving critique. Rubbed correctly iron does sharpen iron.

Chapter 2
Observations, Not Opinions

*N*o evangelistic effort, organization, or Christian revival, has filled more church pews than the fellowship of Alcoholics Anonymous. The count of AA members who are now vital members of their congregations dwarfs the numbers of those who came to faith during the revivals of centuries past, the Great Awakening, or even the modern media-aided crusades of such gifted men as Dr. Billy Graham and others. Despite this obvious truth, the theology exhibited in the famous 12 Steps of AA has been harried by certain Christian denominations and their doctrine police from the fellowship's very inception and it continues today. This should not be so.

Doctrinally-devoted Christians are at a loss to Scripturally explain AA's role as being the first stop for so many who have come to faith in the Bible. One might rightly conclude modern Christian doctrinal "experts" consider the fellowship of Alcoholics Anonymous another tentacle of the "post-modern beast."[7] Granted AA can easily be mistaken for post modernism which, in the name of mass appeal and/or to soothe new cultural senses, has led so many astray through a filtered reading of the Bible.

---

[7] Post modernism is generally ascribed to an ecumenical movement in the United States after World War !! which reduces Scripture by ignoring many of its hard teachings.

Tanking AA with post modernism is the seemingly sound conclusion of religious academics. This should not be so either.

AA's "God as we understand Him" in the third and eleventh steps surely appears to be a post modernism but it's not. We all deal with "God as we understand Him." A room full of the most Reformed divinity students, in complete agreement on doctrine, deal with God as He is understood by each individual. Inarguably, an individual's life experience, interpretation of that life experience and interpretation of other's life experiences, creates individual God-understanding prisms.

Consider this analogy. One friend may describe me and our relationship using different adjectives than another. Their experience with me is different producing a different description and understanding of who I am. Their experience in our relationship might be different but I'm the same person. Experiences with the God of the Bible can be described differently and Scripture not be contradicted. The God of the Bible is understood in as many ways as there are humans to understand Him. God is indeed a personal God.

Of course, the one and only God of the Bible has universally observed characteristics. Just because a friend is talking about a friend doesn't mean he is talking about me. AA professes there is only one God while it seems Biblical theologians assume AA grants license to define God. Step 3 doesn't say "God as we <u>choose</u> to understand Him."

Admittedly, the phrase "God as we understand Him" is a loose noose for the many atheist and agnostic newcomers to AA but the figurative noose tightens neatly in the AA process. While newcomers to AA are encouraged to "knock on the door"[8] with a concept of God they chose, or even conjure, the door opens pretty quick to reveal who really owns the house. Upon examination, Step 3 becomes a sudden hiccup to those making God out to be what they want Him to be. At the end of the day, no one makes a decision to turn their will and life over to Mother Nature or a door knob, not for long anyway. Besides, the AA experience demonstrates undeniably that allowing one to conjure God to make a spiritual start is far less harmful than mandating belief in God portrayed incorrectly. AA mandates only a willingness to believe and an open mind. God doesn't seem to have a problem revealing himself at the time of His choosing. As far as I know God is batting a thousand. God never says "oops, I missed one."

Step 5 "Admitted to God," Step 7, "humbly ask God," and Step 11, "God's will," slips the noose to a pretty tight knot eventually. God is God in AA pretty unambiguously upon close inspection. The AA text's description of God as "Creator"[9] is a clincher. AA sojourners who take license to define God find themselves in a box pretty fast. It has proven to be a harmless box if

---

[8] Matthew 7:7 Jesus said knock and the door will be opened to you.

[9] *Alcoholics Anonymous*, p. 13, 25, 28, 56, 68, 72, 75, 76, 80, 83, 158, 161.

eventually abandoned. The important point is that no part of AA theology denies the deity of Christ and the Steps don't read, "Jesus as we understand Him."

Whatever the reason for criticism, or refusal to engage, or the outright ignoring of the AA phenomenon, the success of Alcoholics Anonymous demands from the intellectually honest Christian theologian an explanation. Unable to curse it because of its success and unable to Scripturally explain the obvious blessing of sobriety in so many, AA leaves Christian theologians in a befuddlement. Is AA Jesus at work or not? The response "Jesus is at work everywhere" is a dishonest dodge. AA's success filling pews and selling Bibles demands a specific answer to this question from any honest proponent of Christian doctrine.

Alcoholics Anonymous is the closest thing to first-century Christianity to appear on planet earth since the time of Christ and the last 85 years prove it's no fad. Also, in the last twenty years American Christendom has experienced a resurgence of Reformed theology. Many of the new mega nondenominational churches feast on the teachings of the sixteenth century Reformed thinkers like Martin Luther, John Calvin and Huldrych Zwingli. Reading the Bible as written is gaining favor in growing congregations. Post modern churches are the ones in financial straights and bleeding congregants. Expressed by the impeccable reasoning of Christian apologist, "Reformed Thought" of today and the principles of Alcoholics Anonymous pass honest, intellectual rigor with equal validity. AA is a walking, talking portrayal of Biblical truth as construed by the Reformed. The Reformed just don't know it.

The author stumbled quite accidentally on the cohesion of AA doctrine and Reformed theology when the latter was explained and experienced through a Bible study curriculum called "Sonship." Seven years of exposure to Alcoholics Anonymous and being raised as a regular attender of a "social" but legalistic, post-modern church made up my spiritual underpinning before Sonship. In AA a miracle had happened to me in the form of a spiritual awakening as the result of the 12 Steps. Paradoxically, a gift of desperation had paid off in complete liberation from substance abuse through the blessing of Alcoholics Anonymous.

But how soon we forget? With God's major miracle seven years in the rearview, The Almighty began to lose His luster in my life. Having the trappings I had gotten sober to get produced an unexpected restlessness and discontentedness. I turned around and life had grown more difficult. My gratitude was seeping out. I was in a new place, in need of spiritual renewal without the motivation of overt desperation. There became an empty spot in my spiritual condition which cried, "there must be more!" and it would not be quieted.

It was in this new place, with an oh-so latent desperation, that a strange spark of attraction (I can take no credit for the decision) led me to a new church in my small university town. The distinction of this church is the congregation's faith in a literal interpretation of Scripture and their Reformed beliefs. I considered a literal reading of Scripture the elixir of the uneducated and the prescription of Christian churches with a thirst for legalism. Modern day Pharisees were to be avoided like the plague by a recovered alcoholic like myself. I perceived their legalistic answer to addiction as the thoroughly disproved "pull-yourself-up-by-your-bootstraps" or "just say 'no' to drugs" approach. Constantly trying and failing to win the favor of my childhood's God as presented by these stiff-necked brethren left me weary, pocked by disobedience and disgusted with their business model.

The people in this new church were led by a pastor who didn't take himself too seriously despite his obvious intellectual abilities.[10] The pastor brought a marked difference in the Sunday worship aurora as well. These people laughed a lot, and frequently at themselves. How refreshing! Disavowing religious fundamentalism and legalism strongly, even calling it sin, was an unexpected tenant of their beliefs and more than a nuance. Though "Reformed" was no more than a word from history at my level of experience, what it meant to these people had me curious from the get-go. The congregants didn't behave as the legalistic fundamentalist I associated with a literal

---

[10] Dr. Timothy S. Lane, who has since authored many books including "Relationships, A Mess Worth Making," was the pastor. He's one awesome dude.

reading of the Bible. Again, far too much laughter and lightheartedness, too much like an AA meeting.

The Pharisees of religious fundamentalism and "doctrinal legalism" are the antithesis of Alcoholic Anonymous and the 12 Steps. My new Reformed friends claimed the "intellectually dishonest" who picked favorite parts of the Bible and trashed the rest as their antithesis along with the legalist who added to Scripture. They used the specific words of "postmodern," or "secular humanist," and "legalist" as pejorative labels for their contrarians. "Postmodernist" was a new category for me but I recognized the identities. AA meetings are held mostly in postmodern church basements (out of necessity not choice).

The fundamentalist, the health and wealth crowd, the cultural Christians (postmodernist), and the Armenian evangelicals, with Catholicism a mainstay, made up the discernible whole of Christendom to my understanding at the time. Had I come upon a new camp? I decided to hang around for awhile and see.

Besides, considering my background was in the spiritual big leagues of Alcoholics Anonymous, my presence would offer a font of wisdom to these "earth people" (AA lingo for non-alcoholics). After all, had I not witnessed many miracles and seen God plainly at work sobering up alcoholics in AA? Where these mere mortals simply opined on miracles past I carried the experience of many firsthand accounts. I represented with vigor the ego mania and pervasive inferiority complex which tends to beleaguer alcoholics, in or out of recovery.

My first acquaintance with this church had truly been an eye-opener. The familiar faces belonged to many I knew to hold post graduate degrees. Still, my AA miracle-witnessing pedigree left me unintimidated and I was sure my spiritual maturity bested theirs. Being the accomplished approval-suck that I am, sharing in Sunday school as though it was an AA meeting got attention and fed my ego nicely. Sharing an observation in Sunday school beginning with, "when I drank liquor," has entertainment value for all. I was having a big time. There was no bridle of potential clients in attendance as hinderance. From the blue-haired ladies to the students from the local university, all were impressed with my courageous honesty. The ability to feed my ego was camouflaged expertly. By the third Sunday the class was standing room only. Not knowing about ego maniacs with inferiority complexes, they didn't suspect a thing; nor did I.

One of the "attracted" in that Sunday school class invited my wife and me to a Bible study she and her husband where hosting that explored the 16 lesson Bible study called "Sonship," written by Dr. C. John (Jack) Miller, a former practical theology professor at Westminster Theological Seminary in Philadelphia. Judging the time commitment to be finite and the driving distance short, we accepted the invitation. The following Tuesday night we gathered to watch the first video of the series led by Dr.

Miller's wife Rosemary and meet our fellow "growth group" seekers.

The introductions were memorable on both counts. Out of ten people who made up the five couples, six held a phd and one was a medical doctor. As an alcoholic insurance salesman I figured God was up to something, subjugating my ego like that and everything. Such a concentration of gray matter had to be respected, even by me. When the video started the first words out of Rosemary's mouth were, "I'm Rosemary Miller and I am a recovering Pharisee." My jaw dropped.

The Sonship material stunned me. This explanation of the Gospel was all new and the principles matched AA's exactly. I had been raised in a supposedly Reformed Presbyterian Church and was the veteran of a thousand AA meetings. How had I missed this incredible intellectual cogency between Scripture and AA? In AA, the 12 Steps are nebulously attributed to the Bible. Sonship's literal reading of Scripture, from the Reformed perspective, mimicked AA dogma fantastically. Sonship magnificently creased my soul and what enveloped that crease is the fountain from which the words of this book flow.

Learning how Alcoholics Anonymous and the 12 Steps not only endure Biblical scrutiny but reaffirmed it was transformative. I began to see that AA miracles confirm the Reformed reading of Scripture. No light shines between Biblical principles and AA principles. I had always thought this to be true but I could never explain the relationship exactly. The Sonship material's explanation was completely new to me and would have been new to my friends in AA. I had never heard this stuff before much less thought about it. For the first time I saw specifically how the two sets of principles are really one. AA principles might best be described as an ingeniously constructed skeleton of Biblical principles. I never understood before there is no "law-keeping" in either.

Concisely, "Reformed Theology" considers the word "chosen" to be indispensable, pivotable actually, in understanding Scripture. In agreement AA literature puts it like this:

*"Those who do not recover are people who cannot or will not completely give themselves to this simple program, usually men and women who are constitutionally incapable of being honest with themselves. There are such unfortunates. **They are not at fault; they seem to have been born that way** (emphasis added). They are **naturally incapable** (emphasis added) of grasping and developing a manner of living which demands rigorous honesty. Many suffer from grave mental and emotional disorders but many of them do recover if they have the capacity to be honest."*[11]

The logically-explained observations of the AA experience contained in this book will hopefully compel Reformed believers to take a look at AA from a "confirming" perspective. Any perceived heresy is just that,

---

[11] *Alcoholics Anonymous*, p. 85

perceived. First century Christians operated without the New Testament. Jesus said plainly, "you will know them by their fruits,"[12] and AA's fruits are not in dispute. AA fruit is pretty darn fruity. Jesus' litmus test sticks in the craw of the Christian doctrine police, the self-assured Reformed believers who think AA doesn't fit their denominational narrative in particular.

Christendom must note, written by an Episcopal clergyman and an alcoholic stockbroker, five of the 12 Steps contain the word "God." To a person, the millions of alcoholics transformed by the 12 Steps, who were once chronically intoxicated and who now live productively sober, credit God with their deliverance. How could Jesus not love the rooms of Alcoholics Anonymous? His kind of people hang out there. Organized religion ignores the proofs of Scripture evident in the rooms of AA at its peril and the peril of their congregants who, plagued by besetting sins of all varieties, suffer the consequences. There is much at stake.

To members of the recovery community, it is hoped this book's insights will spur those who have experienced the "psychic change"[13] and spiritual awakening referenced in the AA literature to further investigation of what the Bible really says about Jesus. After 40 years of being around the rooms of AA, I can assure those in recovery the

---

[12] Matthew 7:16

[13] *Alcoholics Anonymous*, p. 85

Bible doesn't say what you think it says. Taking a "deep dive" into the Bible from this new perspective will mature the AA experience intellectually if not spiritually.

This material seeks to unveil the Bible's really, really big God. Adam's "sin bequeath," the "fall of Man," has left us in need of a really big God. Only a second Adam can logically be of scale to provide the cosmic mulligan required to atone for the first Adam's dastardly desire to be his own God. The Gospel proclaims that indeed a second Adam has appeared and the legions of recovered "12 Steppers" who have experienced a psychic change provide compelling evidence of how thoroughly God can address the issue. Unfortunately, many who have experienced AA's psychic change still stand on the cusp of this understanding due to so much religious prejudice and/or the influence of legalistic Bible reading. Dash the legalism!

Actually, AA demonstrates Jesus is even better than many of the most ardent churchgoers know, can even imagine or, more surprisingly, are willing to accept. What if churchgoers become convinced their sins (defects of character), past, present and future, have really been forgiven? What if shame and guilt were banished as tools used in attempting to bring about forced repentance and hoped-for obedience? Would the forgiven take license to feed their worldly lust? Would their self-will run riot? Would such freedom corrupt? The Scriptures and the AA experience shout, "no!" emphatically.

Sadly, many churchgoers, as well as their critics in AA, completely misunderstand God's law and its purpose. Misunderstanding God's law is the source of untolled pain and lost freedom. We humans crave the deception of finding ourselves to be "good people." We long to feel any flash of comfort we can wring from our own righteousness, our own "goodness." It is not unfair to speculate most churchgoers, along with those matured in AA, consider themselves masters of the Ten Commandments to an acceptable degree. God's grace is poisoned by such awful misconceptions. This book explains the details of how faulty thoughts of "just rewards" for moral uprightness spew an enslaving false righteousness.

Striving to live lives pleasing to God (as opposed to living a life depending on God) trying to earn His grace (or repay Him for it), is slavery. Sucking approval from fellows and accumulating material things to show ourselves righteous or "worthy" are common elements of this "convict code."

In a self-deceiving dance to achieve our own righteousness we find ourselves stuck spiritually. To dance just the right steps to earn God's good favor and pacify His demands of good behavior is the curse hardwired into all sons and daughters of Adam. The "mostly upright" stumble exhaustingly through life. Gripping the self-righteous bars of pride's prison, trying to use will power to stoke a desire to be obedient, or acceptably obedient, we try to manipulate

God into giving us what we want using our behavior. We try to turn God into a lenient Santa Claus.

Never taking the time to understand the illogical nature of these pursuits, we forfeit the sweetness of life. Unliberated descendants of Adam obstinately bear hug the razor blades of self-sufficiency. These blades of self-sufficiency carve the human's conscience into columns of guilt and shame. Our constant failures to please God leave residual angst and uncertainty floating just beneath the surface in our thought-life even when there is no crisis.

Many Christian "treatment centers" today, especially those operated by Christian fundamentalist, advertise a "Biblical approach" to the 12 Steps. The redundancy is not harmless. These addiction treatment protocols use shame and guilt that cruelly push the sufferer deeper into the darkness of addiction. Scripture and the Big Book explain why these "bootstrap" approaches to evoke will power do not yield lasting sobriety and never will. Christian fundamentalist, arrogantly "spinning" to create a "Biblical approach to the 12 Steps," only confirm AA's success and their theology's failures. Turning the12 Steps of AA into some plain old pull-yourself-up-by-your-bootstraps theology is no benign act. Addiction is an epidemic killer. It needs no help.

Fundamentalist, legalistic, "mom and pop" treatment centers, with "mom and pop" protocols, are tragically common across America. Covetously and arrogantly editing to make the 12 Steps Biblical when they are already Biblical, these operations extract a heavy toll upon those who come under their care. Their results are horrifically less than nil. **Addiction is addiction because will power is a completely ineffective solution.**

To successfully argue that "bootstrap" approaches are not Biblical and that AA is Biblical requires a "rule of the road." The supposition must be that the Bible is true and complete. No "reading between the lines," or taking Scripture out of context, no adding or subtracting Scripture allowed. The legitimacy of Scripture's canonization as being Divinely inspired is a different debate. That's another book for different author. Jesus was born of a virgin or he wasn't. Jesus came out of the tomb with the wound of a thrusted sword in His side or he didn't. If Jesus was just another man or great teacher he is history's greatest charlatan. Jesus claimed to be the Messiah and walked around forgiving sins. Jesus "is" or Jesus "ain't."

For those who doubt the inerrancy of Scripture, no matter your stripe, in or out of Alcoholics Anonymous, let the assumption of Scripture as being God-breathed, or *solo scriptura* in the vernacular, be "for the sake of argument" if necessary. No theme of logic must be breached in examining the words of the Bible for legitimacy in light of actual experience. A mere open mind is sufficient for understanding. Forget what you think the Bible says. Reading the Bible's words as written is a journey worth the effort.

Evidence of how paradoxical Biblical truths powerfully transform the lives of alcoholics emanates from in the rooms of AA on a daily basis. From their Reformed constructs, the 12 Steps produce miracles on a grand scale in relative obscurity. The AA experience is an incredibly compelling case for the accuracy of Reformed doctrine's differentiating characteristics. There is much the modern-day church, including the Reformed category, needs to glean from the fellowship meeting in postmodern church basements. Ignoring miracles is a big decision.

The insanity of the alcoholic's first drink is no less perplexing than a believer's choice to seek his own righteousness when Jesus offers the free gift of a superior righteousness. AA doctrine acknowledges an alcoholic's drinking is but a symptom of a condition. Reformed theology proffers the condition is shared by all humanity. There is a God-shaped hole abiding in all humans and we fill it with what works, what provides ease, comfort and an assuaged conscience. The alcoholic's filler of choice is just more readily apparent and therefore more easily examined.

To those in recovery with long-term sobriety, a study of Reformed theology is excitingly useful in explaining what the Bible really says about addiction in regards to God's law (Ten Commandments) and the profoundness of the "Jesus thing." There is even more freedom from shame and guilt available than the Steps can provide, or were intended to provide. AA's 12th Step promises a "spiritual awakening." Presumably the awakened have to roll out of bed at some point! Being open to a little Biblical exploration void of legalism will not detract from realizing an "improved conscious contact with God." I guarantee it.

AA promises those who complete the steps will experience a "fourth dimension"[14] consisting of "a new freedom and a new happiness."[15] AA's fourth dimension is a spiritual "pink cloud." The spiritual tool kit of AA that produces the fourth dimension's pink cloud is described as "the self searching, the leveling of our pride, the confession of shortcomings."[16] Remember, the Big Book was written by those in the "pink cloud" of early sobriety, the most mature barely 4 years into sobriety's journey.

With some simple explanation, the alcoholic with several years of recovery under the belt will immediately recognize the principles illuminated by a close reading of the Gospel. God is due amends, special amends, the ultimate amends. AA promises some awesome things after amends have been made to our fellows in the ninth step.[17] It would not be unreasonable to think there is even greater freedom after amends have been made to God. An attempt to appease God through the 12 Steps, (only admitting one's "character defects," in Step Five) begets something

---

[14] Ibid., p. 25

[15] Ibid., p. 83

[16] Ibid., p. 25

[17] See "The Promises" in Appendix 1

Reformed believers term "cheap grace." Once explained, conceding "cheap grace" caps spiritual growth is no great leap for the open-minded "trudging the road of happy destiny"[18] who are committed to "practicing these principles" in all their affairs.

At the same time Jesus followers need not bemoan the presence of "cheap grace" in AA nor use it in an intellectually dishonest way to classify AA's results as an aberration or unbiblical. The prohibition on "religion" in AA is a strength, not a deficiency. AA has proven conclusively the seeker requires no theology pass the 12 Steps to make a spiritual beginning. This spiritual beginning, more often than not, finds its way to a church pew somewhere.

The 12 Steps address character defects as they pertain to relations with others, not God. AA doctrine addresses "sins" before "Sin." This approach is diametrically opposite the practiced "religious" approach. The church demands one swallow a whole bunch of theology before acting. AA is a program of action first and the results speak for themselves. The 12 Steps allow alcoholics to act their way into right thinking instead of thinking their way into right acting. Chapter Six of the Big Book is entitled "*In To Action*" not "*In To Thinking*" and there's good reason for it.

---

[18] *Alcoholics Anonymous*, p. 164

A Reformed exegesis of the Gospel and AA doctrine demonstrate an earnest look at our individual conditions without the lens of guilt and shame, leads to spiritual growth. Gloriously, the Gospel and AA message concur that it is grace which begets sustainable obedience, not self-fueled, pull-yourself-up-by-your-bootstraps law-keeping. AA and Reformed doctrine aver only love and obedience (sobriety) springing from humility can begin to sufficiently fill the nasty God-shaped void in the human soul.

God's vitalness to our lives, the extent to which we can feel free of guilt, shame and fear, is in direct proportion to our realization of how big our sin problem is and our utter powerlessness over it. If we only have a little sin problem we only need a little God. Both theologies maintain spiritual growth happens when God, not us, gets credit for dealing successfully with our defects of character. Most poignantly, both the Bible and AA acknowledge victory only comes through surrender of our lives to the care of God. Neither is a "self help" program. For the alcoholic, helping ourselves got us into one tiger of a mess.

Recovered alcoholics and churchgoers exploring the majestic, Biblical paradoxes of freedom are brethren on the same journey. The foliage of their spiritual growth is of the same seed.

Chapter 3

Disease And The Law

Second only to the absence of the name "Jesus" in AA literature, or acquiescence to "God as we understand Him" in the AA methodology, is the amount of Christian heartburn over AA's treatment of alcoholism as a disease. Whatever doctrinal issues the Christian may have with the disease concept there is no denying the teaching of history. The disease concept revolutionized the treatment of alcoholism. The heartburn comes from misunderstanding. Without the disease concept AA would have no foundation in the Gospel. However camouflaged, the disease concept is rooted in the most fundamental biblical principle. Hear me out.

When the disease concept is considered in combination with something Reformed believers refer to as "the total depravity of man" its vitalness to AA's success is no longer a mystery. After AA co-founder Bill Wilson's initial failures he changed his tactics to emphasizing the medical properties of alcoholism when talking with Dr. Bob Smith, AA's other co-founder. After some explanation it will be clear why the Apostle Paul would have approved.

The doctrine of man's total depravity is a concept that distinguishes "sin" from "Sin." Succinctly, "sins" are the acts promulgated by our "sin nature." "Sin," capital "S," is our inherited condition. According to the Bible all humans are born with a "sin nature" inherited from Adam. Humans are self-seeking from day one. A two year old child proves it. The "terrible twos" is not learned behavior.

No one chooses to be a "sinner." No one can avoid the moral deficiencies that make one a "sinner." It comes free of charge. In context, no one chooses to be an alcoholic any more than one chooses to be sinner. Conversely, to drink responsibly is the dream of every alcoholic.

Certainly there is no alcoholic bacteria or virus nor, as this is written, is there any genetic marker science can tie to alcoholism. Bill Wilson confessed belief alcoholism wasn't a disease in the traditional since back in 1962. There are, however, traits of alcoholism that inarguably exhibit disease characteristics. The most poignant of these characteristics is that if alcoholism is treated as a disease a beginning in AA, with the probable destination of a church pew, can be made. This is a very, very important point for the purposes of this book. The annuls of human history show treating alcoholism as a moral failing to be of no value in arresting the calamity and mayhem of an alcoholic lifestyle.

The disease concept in AA is used to communicate to the alcoholic the hopelessness of the condition, nothing more. AA literature states unequivocally that alcoholism is a spiritual malady accompanied by the phenomenon of craving at the introduction of alcohol into the body. The term "spiritual" refers to facets of life that affect every nook and cranny of our being. The ancient "Spirits" sign over the liquor store is not false advertising.

Putting aside for the moment concerns regarding any license the disease concept might offer the alcoholic to avoid responsibility can liberate the Christian mind in a particular fashion. By escaping the need to maintain a "culpability" perspective, the disease concept of alcoholism can shine light into one of the most perplexing, yet marvelously wonderful pieces of Scripture- the seventh chapter of Romans. Consider Romans 7:19, *"For I do not do the good I want to do but the evil I do not want to do- this I keep on doing. Now if I do what I do not want to do, it is no longer I who do it, but it is sin living in me that does it."* What Christian worth his salt hasn't noodled on this mystery? Sounds like Paul is describing addiction to me. For sure, no addict would deny Paul's words apply to the malady.

A good working definition of an alcoholic is requisite at this juncture. The fellowship of AA has vast experience testing the wonderfully simplistic definition of an alcoholic contained in the Big Book. An alcoholic is a person who experiences the phenomenon of craving upon feeling the effects of alcohol. Given the opportunity, once the effects of alcohol are felt an alcoholic will not stop drinking until rendered unconscience. Once the phenomenon of craving is triggered by ingesting alcohol, the real alcoholic drinks until passing out. The downfall is not the fourth or fifth drink, it's the first.

This definition encompasses the binge drinker, the alcoholic who may stay sober for a period of time, even years, but once alcohol is introduced moderation never happens. The amount of alcohol is not the determining factor in AA's definition of an alcoholic. The metric is the person's response to the effects of alcohol.

Observationally, this phenomenon of "craving" in alcoholics reveals there is some type of abnormal reaction to the chemical properties of alcohol by some and not others. Statistics show about 6.2% of people over 18 in the U.S. suffer from Alcohol Use Disorder (AUD).[19] That's over 18 million suffers. I think we can all agree antidotally the condition is known to have a hereditary aspect.

Science and the law consider alcoholism attributable to a chemical imbalance in the brain. The medical community recognizes that alcoholism presents itself just like a mental illness or form of insanity. AA's second step concurs using the carefully selected words "restore us to sanity." It is worth noting AA came to this conclusion some 40 years before the American Medical Association.

AA literature takes great pains to describe "heavy drinkers" who, if presented sufficient reason to do so, can arrest a destructive drinking pattern on their own. Should a person need to know whether they are an alcoholic or a

---

[19] National Institute on Alcohol and Alcoholism, 2017

heavy drinker a simple experiment can make the distinction. Make 24 beers available to the subject in question to be consumed over 12 days, two beers per day. The heavy drinker might be able to drink two beers a day for 12 days. The alcoholic cannot no matter the consequences. Even to get health restored, family problems solved or realize financial security, the alcoholic cannot drink two beers a day for 12 days. No evidence hints the alcoholic could pass such a test under threat of death.

Think an alcoholic has no willpower? Let an alcoholic trigger the phenomenon of craving by feeling the effects of alcohol and the most incredible examples of the human will can be observed in the acquisition of more alcohol. The alcoholic's ingenuity in this regard is legendary. To cure the morning shakes, the far-gone alcoholic will drink and throw up until that first drink stays down. The alcoholic's willpower to drink is a force of nature, or sin nature as it were.

The field of medicine is well acquainted with this "craving" aspect of alcoholism. Sufficiently saturated and denied alcohol, an alcoholic will experience delirium tremors, or DTs, upon abstinence. Withdrawal from alcohol kills people every day. Can you think of another "sin," where cessation brings death? Me either. This is a unique feature of alcoholism that points to the abnormal effects of alcohol's chemical properties on the brain of alcoholics.

Make no mistake, the alcoholic drinks because of a love for the effects produced by alcohol. Once the effects of alcohol fill the God-shaped hole in an alcoholic, using such an effective, readily-available coping mechanism is understood logically, if not chemically. The need to fill our God-shaped hole, Adam's tyrannical legacy, is not subject to self-denial. Once a person has crossed that line into active alcoholism delaying gratification by not using alcohol is simply not a viable option. The alcoholic doesn't have a drinking problem. An alcoholic has a drinking solution.

    Most alcoholics recovering in AA, or recovered using the 12 Steps, recall feeling the effects of alcohol for the first time as a seminal event in their lives. Most recount a filling of their God-shaped hole immediately. Experiencing such a magnificent coping mechanism that works so dependably erodes any contention that continuing the practice of coping using alcohol is a run-of-the-mill moral decision. Many cross the line from heavy drinker to alcoholism very early in their drinking careers- many claim on the first day.

    Experience also shows self-knowledge that one is an alcoholic has absolutely no ability to prevent unbridled, constant drunkenness or even kickstart recovery. To a certain extent, alcoholism is a self-diagnosed condition but the self-diagnosis holds no power. Many interpersonal wars have been waged to break through a person's alcoholic denial. Having lost the battle and finally forced to admit to being an alcoholic, the vanquished spitefully toasts the shame and guilt of their adversary's triumph. The faulty pretense is that the alcoholic lacks knowledge. That there is no power in self-knowledge is a monster clue regarding the nature of addiction. Lack of power, not will power, not self-knowledge, is the alcoholic's dilemma.

The Big Book of AA makes this accurate and informative analogy. Reflect on Paul's words in Romans 7 as you read about the Big Book's metaphorical jaywalker:

"Our behavior is as absurd and incomprehensible with respect to the first drink as that of an individual with a passion, say, for jay-walking. He gets a thrill out of skipping in front of fast-moving vehicles. He enjoys himself for a few years in spite of friendly warnings. Up to this point you would label him as a foolish chap having queer ideas of fun. Luck then deserts him and he is slightly injured several times in succession. You would expect him, if he were normal, to cut it out. Presently he is hit again and this time has a fractured skull. Within a week after leaving the hospital a fast-moving trolley car breaks his arm. He tells you he has decided to stop jay-walking for good, but in a few weeks he breaks both legs.

On through the years this conduct continues, accompanied by his continual promises to be careful or to keep off the streets altogether. Finally, he can no longer work, his wife gets a divorce and he is held up to ridicule. He tries every known means to get the jaywalking idea out of his head. He shuts himself up in an asylum, hoping to mend his ways. But the day he comes out he races in front of a fire engine, which breaks his back. Such a man would be crazy, wouldn't he?

You may think our illustration is too ridiculous. But is it? We, who have been through the wringer, have to admit if we substituted alcoholism for jay-walking, the illustration would fit exactly. However intelligent we may have been in other respects, where alcohol has been involved, we have been strangely insane. It's strong language but isn't it true?

Some of you are thinking: "Yes, what you tell us is true, but it doesn't fully apply. We admit we have some of these symptoms, but we have not gone to the extremes you fellows did, nor are we likely to, for we understand ourselves so well after what you have told us that such things cannot happen again. We have not lost everything in life through drinking and we certainly do not intend to. Thanks for the information."

That may be true of certain nonalcoholic people who, though drinking foolishly and heavily at the present time, are able to stop or moderate, because their brains and bodies have not been damaged as ours were. But the actual or potential alcoholic, with hardly any exception, will be absolutely unable to stop drinking on the basis of self-knowledge. This is a point we wish to emphasize and re-emphasize, to smash home upon our alcoholic readers as it has been revealed to us out of bitter experience.[20]

History is replete with highly functioning alcoholics of extreme intelligence and amazing abilities who are able

---

[20] *Alcoholics Anonymous*, p. 37-39

to exert great will power in other areas of their lives. Lack of power is the alcoholic's perplexity (just like every descendant of Adam incidentally). Don't be confused. An alcoholic can quit drinking. Suffering terrible regret and remorse many quit every day. The issue is staying quit. Alcoholics do not do the good they want to do but the evil they do not want to do- this they keep on doing. Paul's words fit exactly.

Despite the devastating consequences of using alcohol as a coping substance, alcoholics take a first drink with the notion or vague hope that "it's going to be different this time." The experience of countless members of AA demonstrates an alcoholic suffers from a strange mental twist preventing an extrapolation of the first drink's consequences. The horrible aftermath so predictable when an alcoholic drinks mysteriously is not a controlling thought in the brain of an alcoholic. The Big Book puts it bluntly: for the spiritually unfit alcoholic "there is no mental defense against that first drink."[21] The popular definition of insanity as repeating the same behavior and expecting a different result originated in AA.

The vast majority of alcoholics who stop drinking long enough to engage the 12 Steps do so because of relationship, legal, or health (lover, lawyer or liver) problems; or because, inexplicably, alcohol suddenly no longer fills up the God-shaped hole. No one has ever

---

[21] Ibid., p. 43

showed up to the rooms of AA ready to take the Steps with a manageable life and a desire to stop drinking born of an exercise in intellectual reasoning or the dawning of good judgment. Experience shows conclusively that the gift of desperation is indispensable and understanding one suffers from an incurable condition is the only piece of self-knowledge of any value. After reading this book why this is true will make perfect sense.

AA success stories demonstrate, without exception, when one endeavors to get well instead of obedient miracles can happen. Surrender resides in the notion of getting well. Resolving to be more obedient is just a counterpunch. Counterpunches never land. Five thousand years of experience dealing with addiction did prove one thing- throwing counterpunches at addiction is a bloody fight that never ends.

Churchgoers seem to carry a visceral obligation to deny the disease characteristics of addiction. Fearing acknowledgement to the alcoholic of a situation unable to be addressed by will power, the conclusion is that such an acknowledgement is a license for the alcoholic to drink. "Don't tell the alcoholic he is powerless over his craving for alcohol! He'll just give up trying to be sober and be drunk all the more!" Like the practicing alcoholic needs any permission to achieve the greatest level of intoxication possible at any given opportunity?! Really?!

I wonder how many churchgoers understand Romans chapter seven, when Paul cries, *"it is not me that sins but sin that lives in me!"* I wonder if they would have accused Paul of trying to dodge responsibility.

Even more outrageously Paul identifies "the law" as the culprit when we don't *"do the good we want to do."* Romans 7:5 *"the sinful passions aroused <u>by the law</u> are at work."* I wonder how many churchgoers know the Bible claims "sinful passions" are "aroused by the law." I went to church for 38 years without a single soul telling me the law aroused sinful passions. I missed that Sunday.

How the disease concept acts in conjunction with the 12 Steps to thwart "the law-keeping" and keep it from arousing the "sinful passions" in alcoholics is a key insight of this book. How the law works to arouse our sin nature is right there in the Bible. Much more on this later. For now, suffice to say the disease concept is used in AA to take the alcoholic out from under the law as it pertains to abusing alcohol.

No amount of a person's will power is going to elevate total depravity. No amount of a person's will power is going to keep "the law" from arousing sinful passions. Whether alcoholism is a disease or not is beside the point. The point is that considering the sin nature from the perspective of the disease concept works when it comes to alcoholism.

Why the disease concept is not used in Scripture for illustration is a fair question. The author speculates that to have done so would have sold Sin short. In reality Sin is much more encompassing than any disease. Some diseases can be cured. It must be acknowledged however, that our "flawed genetics" that come from Adam is not only an aspect of Sin described in Scripture, it is the foundation. To say the disease concept is not used in the Bible is not entirely correct.

  AA uses the disease concept to mimic the most fundamental part of the Gospel. In fact, we will see how the disease concept ties AA inextricably to the Gospel to the exclusion of any other religion. How AA and the Bible use the same approach to this mystery of how the law arouses sinful desires is a profound understanding. Fully explaining the elements needed for understanding this mystery first requires some context.

Chapter 4
Two Histories

*M*uch perspective can be gained by understanding the origin of a thing. The relationship between the belief systems of Reformed theology and Alcoholics Anonymous are better understood after knowing a bit about what "provoked" the genesis of each. Both were a response to the failures of legalism. A short review might extinguish much prejudice and dissipate a good amount of misunderstanding, particularly with regard to Christian angst over perceived AA heresies.

<u>The Reformation Briefly</u>

Vast volumes have been written on the origins and development of Reformed Christian thought, all of which are unneeded here. A brief snippet will do.

After some five hundred years the Reformation still profoundly influences our daily lives. Certain aspects of the Reformation's story are particularly meaningful to any member of AA who has experienced a psychic change and spiritual awakening as the result of the 12 Steps. Those who have been enlightened from the darkness of the why-can't-you-drink-like-a-normal-person puzzlement will be vitally interested in certain aspects of "Reformed" history.

The Reformation's origin is dated to the early 1500s. Western Civilization, Europe by geography, was emerging from the Dark Ages. The plague was discovered to be carried by fleas on rodents, Columbus had recently discovered America, Magellan was circumnavigating the globe, gunpowder started being used in guns, and, most importantly, the invention of the printing press was coming into its own. Gutenberg's 1455 invention of the printing press in Frankfurt, Germany, is rightly considered the seminal developmental event of the second millennium. It took the internet 500 years to rival the magnitude of the printing press' impact on society.

The printing press not only changed the cost of disseminating information but more importantly it changed the way people thought about disseminating information. It became obvious that control over information had been lost to large extent. The leap was quantum. At this new price point the illiterate, which was practically the entire population, became interested in becoming literate. The printing press changed everything. This point in history was a really good time to change folk's minds about some deeply held religious beliefs which had "evolved" over time.

The Pope was, for all intents and purposes, the Church. His monopoly on Christendom in Western Civilization was complete, and unthreatened, until the printing press. Local church authorities, empowered by the Pope's political position and endowed with the requisite authority of the Pope, reigned over their allotted pieces of terra firma. Religious power transcended political power. Reading the Bible, in Latin, to the illiterate faithful had lucrative advantages. The setup left the population at the mercy of some dubious characters and their influence over European daily life was immense. The church's power over society is hard to comprehend today.

Of course, the Church, and those running it, enjoyed the economic benefits and political power that came with this societal influence. The Church, in addition to its spiritual obligations regarding the sacraments, was executing a very lucrative business plan. Being able to legalistically add to Scripture came in handy.

The Church in Rome used its singularly expansive distribution network to market "indulgences." Rome's perpetration of this fraud marked the crest of Christian history's greatest "works righteousness" movement since the Pharisees handed Jesus and his message that righteousness comes through faith over to Pilate for crucifixion.

The Pope just finally dispensed of "working" for righteousness to satisfy the sinner's side of the *quid pro quo* with God by putting a price tag on forgiveness of different sins; committed, planned or unplanned. Purgatory could be avoided by paying a price to view relics or have the right prayers said by the right people. For a fee, the priest would say the necessary prayers of absolution and square everything with the Man Upstairs as only he could. For the right price one could even have the dearly departed prayed out of hell or purgatory, as the case required. Being a priest was good work if you could get it.

One of these priest, Martin Luther, tortured by his own conscience, seeing at least a speck of his sin in his every effort and motive, mustered the gumption to post his "Ninety Five Theses" to the door of his German church in 1517. Not coincidently this church was right down the road from where the printing press was changing the world. God is truly an efficient God. The combination of these 95 ideas and the printing press meant "game on" for the Pope and his business plan.

Luther's Ninety Five Theses called out the Pope on the immorality of this indulgence business and promoted fervently a return to the doctrine of righteousness by faith and faith alone. Luther, the rambunctious outlier with access to a printing press, wreaked havoc on the Church's influence and its business model. The Pope summarily gave Martin Luther the boot in 1520 issuing a papal bull giving Luther 60 days to recant and ordered all his books burned. In retaliation, Luther burned the bull and a copy of the cannon of the law right in downtown Wittenberg. (Give humans a printing press and we start burning each other's ideas. It's what humans do.) This split in the Christian church across Western Civilization created Protestants and Catholics.

Characterized by a strict adherence to Scripture, or *solo scriptura*, as opposed to a papal expanded interpretation, the new understanding of God's grace and Christ's atonement for sin morphed Western Civilization.

In the latter part of the sixteenth century, to clear the church of "heresies," (keep economic and political power), Rome sanctioned "inquisitions" to burn people at the stake for making suggestions like the earth rotated around the sun. *Solo scriptura* stood in stark contrast to indulgences and inquisitions, neither of which are in the Bible. Populations under the influence of inquisitions lost influence to populations governed by the inherent freedom of Reformed doctrine.

The resulting liberation from Rome's "works righteousness" theology and savage inquisitions, spawned the greatest advancements in science and the most spectacular creation of art, in volume and brilliance, the world has ever seen. No longer did men of inspiration face the threat of death or economic penalty should a group of priest determine them heretics. This freedom birthed the scientific method which increased the world's collective knowledge exponentially. Artistic expression bloomed. Though The Renaissance was under way, and certainly facilitated the Reformation in important ways, Reformed theology fed the Renaissance as gas to a fire.

Martin Luther's courageous presentation before the Diet of Worms in 1521 along with his commentary on Galatians published in 1535 influenced Europe's greatest minds profoundly. Johann Sebastian Bach spent his professional life working in the early Lutheran Church.

John Locke, the great 17th century philosopher and proponent of religious tolerance, was heavily influenced by Luther's "Priesthood of all Believers." Locke constructed a philosophy of societal justice that dominates Western juris prudence to this day. The words propounding that citizens are "endowed by their Creator with certain unalienable Rights" found in the Declaration of Independence and the Constitution's "We the people" are ideas that came straight from Locke and the Reformation.

The earth-shattering idea in Luther's 95 Thesis was that Scripture stated in no uncertain terms that salvation came through faith not works. The idea one was saved by grace and not works impacted the day to day human thought-life of Western Civilization with a force that can't be overstated. Living in the multimedia 24 hour news cycle's information loop of the twenty first century it's hard to comprehend how radical this idea was and how profoundly it changed the course of human events. People in the 16th century didn't think about a lot of different stuff. One new insight could change everything.

Of course, humans being humans, those liberated from Rome began to diverge into different denominations and fight among themselves. When England's King Henry VIII broke from Rome in 1533 to get his first marriage annulled another slice of The Reformation found its way into the mix. The arguments centered as much around how the church was to be governed as any adherence to a particular flavor of doctrine. Rome's vacuum filled chaotically. The varieties of Protestant denominations, with their variations of church government (church polity) and their tweak on *solo scriptura* is a long, long list. That God has chosen to reveal himself in many different ways is irrefutably in evidence.

At the end of the day, even the Catholics found their footing. Catholicism's influence today is still a mighty thing without the sell of indulgences. This recounting of history is no knock on the Catholics of today. The Reformers' revolt against the Church's legalism was inspired in large part by the writings of good Catholics like Saint Augustine and Thomas Aquinas. Luther and Calvin were just uncompromising when it came to the supremacy of Scripture, or *solo scriptura*. The Scripture's and AA's attitude regarding confession is more Catholic than Protestant for sure.

Today, Reformed thought is contradicted by Arminianism, not Catholicism particularly. Generally speaking, Bible believers fall into one of two camps, Reformed or Armenian. Armenians are legalist and associated with the doctrine of man's "free will." The Reformed are grace centered and associated with the doctrine that righteousness comes through faith given by God. Though Reformed thought survives in many churches, the Presbyterians, the Lutherans and, to some extent the Episcopalians, are historically most closely associated with the much maligned and misunderstood doctrines of predestination and justification. Calvinism, named after the profoundly influential French reformer John Calvin, encompasses Reformed beliefs summarily and is found in many denominations to varying degrees.

The Reformation's birth of Reformed theology was a return to reading the Bible as it was written. There are Protestants who put the Catholics to shame when it comes to love of "works righteousness." Arminianism has Dutch origins and its legalistic doctrines have overwhelmed Protestant seminaries. Legalism is a relentless monster. The important point is that Luther's "righteousness through faith" revolt against legalism spawned the greatest cultural and scientific advancements of the Renaissance. The freedom to make these advancements came under grace not under law. History proves grace has hidden, mystical powers to birth freedom.

The Origins of Alcoholics Anonymous

In 1935 an alcoholic stockbroker named Bill Wilson had a sudden spiritual experience while committed to a New York City psychiatric ward. Subsequently, this shell of a man was to collaborate with Dr. Sam Shoemaker, an Episcopal clergyman, to draft the 12 Steps of Alcoholic Anonymous. A mysterious way of God not even the most fanatical optimist could have suspected used the most unlikely men to bring hope into the hopeless world of addiction.

Wilson, an army officer in World War I and successful investor in the stock market's hay day of the

1920s, had descended into chronic alcoholism by the mid 1930s. His alcoholism required he be committed to several psychiatric hospitals as his condition progressively worsened. Committing chronic alcoholics to asylums, sanitariums and psychiatric wards was the de facto protocol of the day, and the preceding five thousand years for that matter. Bill Wilson's last such stint was at the Towns Psychiatric Hospital in New York City. He committed himself.

Just days prior to Bill's last admission to the psychiatric ward he was visited by an old drinking buddy, Ebby Thacher, who "had gotten religion" through an organization called the Oxford Groups. Originating in England, The Oxford Groups evangelized the skid rows of America's northeastern cities with a Christian message which included complete abstinence. Though each meeting ended with the practiced alter call (one of which Bill answered) and each message was Christ-centered with a very strong Armenian bent, the Oxford Groups' proselytizing had a distinctive "innovation."

The Oxford Group's approach to salvation (not designed to address alcoholism singularly) emphasized complete surrender, private confession of particular sins, restitution to those harmed and service to others. The distinguishing aspect of the approach, the one Thacher so consequentially shared with Bill Wilson, proffered that to make a spiritual beginning prayers could be made to "God as one understood Him." When approached with such a proposition all the tired debate points Wilson mastered over the years were voided.

Bill Wilson always prefaced the story of his Towns Hospital miracle by recounting the day Ebby broached him with the notion of considering "God as he understood God." Bill came to consider God without having to swallow any theology, or minimum theology. The supposition opened a tightly fastened door in the spirit of AA's co-founder.

Many Christians will be very surprised to learn how AA came about. The miracle is an under-told story, even in the rooms of AA today. In the book, *"AA Comes of Age"* Bill Wilson describes what happen in the Townes Hospital and how it led to the creation of Alcoholics Anonymous. Bill Wilson's story, as published in *"AA Comes of Age,"* is 22 years old at its telling:

"I was not in too awful a condition. In three or four days I was free of what little sedative they gave me, but I was very depressed. I was still chewing on the God business. Bright and early one morning my friend Ebby showed up and stood in the doorway, smiling broadly. I didn't see what was so funny. Then I had a suspicion: maybe this is the day he is going to evangelize me; maybe he is going to pour on the sweetness and light. But no, he made me wait until I asked him. "Well," said I, "what is your neat little formula once more?" In perfectly good humor, he handed it out again: You admit you are licked; you're honest with yourself; you talk it out with somebody

else; you make restitution to the people you have harmed; you try to give of yourself without stint, with no demand for reward, and you pray to whatever God you think there is, even as an experiment. It was as simple and yet as mysterious as that. After some small talk he was gone.

My depression deepened unbearably and finally it seemed to me as though I were at the very bottom of the pit. I still gaged badly on the notion of a Power greater than myself, but finally, just for the moment, the vestige of my proud obstinacy was crushed. All at once I found myself crying out, "If there is a God, let Him show Himself! I am ready to do anything, anything!"

Suddenly the room lit up with a great white light. I was caught up into an ecstasy which there are no words to describe. It seemed to me, in the mind's eye, that I was on a mountain and that a wind not of air but of spirit was blowing. And then it burst upon me that I was a free man. Slowly the ecstasy subsided. I lay on the bed, but now for a time I was in another world, a new world of consciousness. All about me and through me there was a wonderful feeling of Presence, and I thought to myself, **"So this is the God of the preachers!"** *(emphasis added). A great peace stole over me and I thought, "No matter how wrong things seem to be, they are still all right. Things are all right with God and His world."*

Then, little by little, I began to be frightened. My modern education crawled back and said to me, "You are hallucinating. You had better get the doctor." Dr.

Silkworth asked me a lot of questions. After a while he said, "No, Bill, you are not crazy. There has been some basic psychological or spiritual event here. I've read about these things in the books. Sometimes spiritual experiences do release people from alcoholism." Immensely relieved, I fell again to wondering what actually happened.

More light on this came the next day. It was Ebby, I think, who brought me a copy of William James' Varieties of Religious Experience. *It was rather difficult reading for me, but I devoured it from cover to cover. Spiritual experiences, James thought, could have objective reality; almost like gifts from the blue, they could transform people. Some were sudden brilliant illuminations; others came on very gradually. Some flowed out of religious channels; others did not. But nearly all had the great common denominators of pain, suffering, calamity. Complete hopelessness and deflation at depth were almost always required to make the recipient ready. The significance of all this burst upon me. Deflation at depth- yes that was it. Exactly that had happened to me. Dr. Carl Jung had told an Oxford Group friend of Ebby's how hopeless his alcoholism was and Dr. Silkworth had passed the same sentence upon me. Then Ebby, also an alcoholic, had handed me the identical dose. On Dr. Silkworth's say- so alone maybe I would never have completely accepted the verdict, but when Ebby came along and one alcoholic began to talk to another, that clinched it.*

Two Histories

My thoughts began to race as I envisioned a chain reaction among alcoholics, one carrying this message and these principles to the next. More than I could ever want anything else, I now knew that I wanted to work with other alcoholics.

As soon as I was discharged from the hospital, I associated myself with the Oxford Groups. We worked at Sam Shoemaker's Calvary Mission and also at Towns Hospital. Ebby came to live with Lois and me in Brooklyn. I started out after drunks on jet propulsion.

My sudden spiritual experience, however, had its disadvantages. I was soon heard to say that I was going to fix up all the drunks in the world, even though the batting average on them had been virtually nil for the last 5,000 years. The Oxford Groupers had tried, had mostly failed, and were fed up. Sam Shoemaker in fact had just had a run of bad luck. He had housed a batch of drunks in an apartment near his church, and one of them, still resisting salvation, had peevishly thrown a shoe through a fine stained-glass window in Sam's church.

No wonder my Oxford Group friends felt that I had better forget about alcoholics. But I was still mighty cocksure and I ignored their advice. Mine was a kind of twin-engine power drive consisting of one part genuine spirituality and one part of my old desire to be a Number One man. This posture didn't pan out well at all. At the end of six months nobody had sobered up. And, believe me, I had tried them by the score. They would clear up for a little while and then flop dismally. Naturally the Oxford Groupers became very cool indeed toward my drunk-fixing.

Lois meanwhile was still working in the department store, and folks were beginning to say, "is the fellow Bill going to be a missionary for life? Why doesn't he go to work?" Even to me, this began to look like a good idea. I began to hang around Wall Street again and, through a chance acquaintance I had scraped up in a brokerage shop, I insinuated myself into a proxy row that involved control of a little machine tool company in Akron, Ohio. In May of 1935 a party of us went out to Akron, fighting for control of the company. I could already see myself as its new president. But when the chips were down the other side had more proxies and our side got licked. My newfound acquaintances were discouraged, and they left me in Akron's Mayflower Hotel with only about ten dollars in my pocket.

They departed on Friday. On Saturday, Mother's Day eve, I was pacing up and down the hotel lobby, wondering what I could do. The bar at one end of my beat was filling up rapidly. I could hear the familiar buzz of conversation in there. Down at the other end of the lobby I found myself pausing before a church directory. Then I was seized with a thought: I am going to get drunk. Or no, maybe I won't get drunk; maybe I'll just go into that bar and drink some ginger ale and scrape up an acquaintance. Then I panicked as never before at the *threat of alcohol. Maybe this meant that my sanity had been restored. I remembered that in trying to help other people, I had stayed sober myself. For the first time I deeply realized it. The thought, "You need another alcoholic to talk to. You need another alcoholic just as much as he needs you!"*

Then followed a strange chain of consequences. Choosing at random from the church directory, I called up an Episcopal padre by the name of Walter Tunks, a great friend of A.A. to this day. In frantic eagerness I poured out my tale to him. I asked if maybe he knew some people who could put me in touch with another alcoholic. I thought he might know some of the Oxford Groupers around Akron. When the good man learned that I was an alcoholic looking for another alcoholic to work on, he at first apparently envisioned two people drunk instead of one, but he finally got the point and gave me a list of about ten people who might be able to direct me.

I immediately began calling them up. It was Saturday afternoon. People were not at home. Others were not interested and made excuses. The list quickly dwindled until it came down to one name at the very end. That name was Henrietta Seiberling. I had a vague recollection from my Wall Street days of meeting an elderly Mr. Seiberling, one-time founder and president of Goodyear Rubber. I could hardly imagine calling up his wife and telling her that I was a drunk from New York looking for another drunk to work on. So I went back downstairs and walked up and down the lobby some more. But something kept saying to me, "You'd better call her." So I finally rang up. Unexpectedly, a young Southern voice came over the wire, which turned out to be that of a Seiberling daughter-in-law. I explained that I was an alcoholic from the New York Oxford Groups who needed to help another drunk in order to stay sober himself. Very quickly she got the drift of what I was saying. She said, "I'm no alcoholic, but I've had my difficulties. When you talk about spiritual matters, I think I understand. I know someone you might help. Won't you come out right away? I live in the gatehouse of the Seiberling place."

When I got there I found a person of charm and understanding. She said she had worked through many a hard problem and had found her answers in the Oxford Groups. She understood deep suffering. When I had told my story she said, "I know just the man for you. He is a doctor. We all call him 'Dr. Bob.' His wife, Anne, is a grand person. Bob has tried so hard; I know he wants to stop. He has tried medical cures, he has tried various religious approaches, including the Oxford Groups. He tried with all his will, but somehow he cannot seem to do it. So how would you like to talk to Dr. Bob and Anne?"

Soon Anne S. was on the phone-AA's much loved Anne. Quickly Henrietta told her about me, an alcoholic from New York who wanted to talk about his drinking problem. Could she and Dr. Bob come over? Anne said,

"I'm sorry, Henrietta. I don't think we can make it today. Bob always makes a great fuss over me on Mother's Day. He has just come home, bringing a big potted plant." What Anne didn't say was that the plant was on a table and that Bob was under the table, so potted that he couldn't get up. Henrietta said, "What about tomorrow? Why can't both of you come over to dinner?" Anne said they would try to make it. Next afternoon at five o'clock that wonderful couple, Dr. Bob and Anne, stood at Henrietta's open door.

This was to be the man who was to be my partner and founder of Akron's Group Number One. With the remarkable Sister Ignatia, he was to care for 5,000 cases of alcoholism in the time when A.A. was still very young. This was the wonderful friend with whom I was never to have a hard word. This was Dr. Bob, A.A's co-founder-to-be."[22]

Bill Wilson and Dr. Bob Smith (affectionately Dr. Bob) leaned heavily on the Oxford Groups in the beginning but soon their philosophies could not coexist. The Oxford Groups' legalistic approach of attempting to channel desperation into a self-effort-fueled pursuit of "absolute purity," "absolute honesty," "absolute unselfishness" and "absolute love," bristled alcoholics trying to recover using AA's 12 Steps.

---

[22] *AA Comes of Age*, (Alcoholics Anonymous World Services, Inc., 1950) p. 62-67

The self-effort element, or the Armenian element, of the Oxford Groups' theology was antithetical to the AA recovery process. AA's philosophy as outlined in the 12 Steps, Step 7 in particular, was a square peg in the Oxford Group's round hole. AA philosophy as exhibited in the seventh step's reliance on God to remove shortcomings and the "practice these principles in all our affairs" edict of AA's twelfth step reflected a "progress not perfection" understanding in AA. This put AA and the Oxford Groups critically at odds over the issue of legalism. The Oxford Groups' penchant for participating in temperance movements was an overt legalism the AA founders rejected uncompromisingly.

There is great irony in the Reformed precepts of AA springing from the overly legalistic doctrines of the Oxford Groups just as the Reformers sprang from the Church's legalism. God does work in many mysterious ways. The essential elements of Reformed theology incorporated into the AA protocol precluded AA from flourishing in The Oxford Groups. The Oxford Groups turned political. The squabbles and general lack of unity destroyed the organization from within.

After many, many failures, at the urging of Dr. William Silkworth (Bill's doctor at Town's Hospital), Bill tried a new approach with Dr. Bob. By emphasizing the disease characteristics of an alcoholic's condition, Bill was able to communicate the presence of a distinctive hopelessness to Dr. Bob, a man of medicine. Leading with the disease concept was an incredibly important development in Bill's strategy. Believing his progress had been fueled by experiencing utter hopelessness and complete nullification of any notion an alcoholic might be able to drink normally again, Bill made a medical pitch. It worked. After a few slips, on June 10, 1935, Dr. Bob took his last drink. He died sober in 1950.

From this auspicious beginning an unparalleled body of evidence regarding the nature of the alcoholic condition and the spiritual "protocol" necessary for recovery evolved quickly. The meeting between Bill and Dr. Bob saved Bill from the drink. Upon this foundation AA's spiritual solution started to achieve success. Bill's efforts proved that an alcoholic could stay sober "witnessing" to another alcoholic. The Bible's "Great Commission" was demonstrated to benefit the witness as much as, if not more than, the one hearing the testimony. Subsequent chapters will demonstrated why this is so and how profound Bill's discovery turned out to be.

Though Bill and Dr. Bob struggled at first, soon a another alcoholic in Akron, Bill D. got sober and stayed that way. There is a famous painting of Bill and Dr. Bob explaining the hopelessness of the alcoholic condition to Bill D. in his hospital room. Dr. Bob, the stalwart, influential, devout Christian of early AA, is holding an open Bible in his lap. Scripture was the literature of early AA meetings. The book Alcoholics Anonymous was not published until 1939. The 12 Steps were not used until the fellowship was well into the journey.

With the addition of Bill D., soon the Akron group was up and running. Meetings were held in Anne and Dr. Bob's home where they lived with Bill until it came time for Bill to return to New York. After a rocky start in New York, a small group took hold. Bill and his wife Lois took in many homeless alcoholics but soon learned that an alcoholic's dependence on them was a detriment to their recovery. There were scores of failures and a few successes but many lessons learned. The primary lesson learned was that nothing secured sobriety as effectively as one alcoholic working with another alcoholic. When all else failed helping another alcoholic carried the day.

Ironically, it wasn't the New York or Akron groups which provided the most potent seed of AA proliferation. A member of the Akron group moved to Cleveland and it was from this group that the veracity of AA's methodology became evident. Alcoholics were getting sober sharing the 12 Steps without Dr. Bob and/or Bill on scene. With the indispensable credibility of significant sobriety happening in the Cleveland group, the AA membership decided a book was in order.

Much debate among this early crew produced the first 164 pages of the book *Alcoholics Anonymous*. Bill Wilson, always the promoter, decided 164 pages would never bring the price he plan to charge for the book so testimonies of selected members were used to add pages of content. That's why the fatten product is known the world over as "The Big Book of Alcoholics Anonymous," or simply "the Big Book" for short.

Wilson had big plans for AA. He saw a chain of hospitals and a stack of money in the offing. Fortunately, other members of AA (Dr. Bob in particular) and John D. Rockefeller nixed those plans. Upon hearing the "AA pitch," Mr. Rockefeller immediately understood power and prestige to be AA land mines. Mr. Rockefeller (a staunch, legalistic, Armenian Christian) was very wise. His enthusiastic support included only a small, judicious amount of funding.

As newly sober AA members moved to new locales across America the fellowship began to grow. Several media articles written in the 1940s produced significant inquiries to the small New York General Services office but one article catapulted AA to institutional status.

In April 1950, the Saturday Evening Post published an article on AA written by investigative journalist Jack Anderson. The response deluged the small staff in New York. Overnight AA was recognized as the lone source of hope for America's masses of suffering alcoholics and their families. An initial skeptic, Mr. Anderson described what he had witnessed in some straightforward reporting. Hopeless alcoholics, low-bottom drunks, were getting sober and that was big, big news in 1950.

The New York office painstakingly answered every inquiry that flowed in as a result of the Saturday Evening Post article. An explosion of grace happened, an incredible explosion of grace. Today it is taken for granted that some can recover from addiction and that many do. Before 1950 no such hope existed. The before and after of Alcoholics Anonymous are the two different eras in the treatment of addiction. As cited, the first era lasted some five thousand years.

Today there are over 70,000 AA groups in the U.S. and Canada with a membership of over 1.4 million. Worldwide there are over 120,000 AA groups with a total membership of 3.5 million people. Over the last 85 years it is estimated that some 64 million people have realized a significant measure of sobriety through the fellowship of Alcoholics Anonymous. If, as the Big Book encourages, half landed in a church somewhere, AA's result is an unmatched evangelistic success. Such a phenomenon must be the work of Almighty God.

Bill Wilson died January 24, 1971, having taken his last drink December 11, 1934.

Chapter 5
A Legal Background

$\mathcal{S}$even years of intensely studying and attempting to practice the principles called for in the program of Alcoholics Anonymous changed everything about my life. The way I perceived myself, the way I perceived God, the world, and my role in it, all became new. AA's promise of a "psychic change" happened to me. My DNA was seemingly altered. The change felt that deep. God removed any desire to abuse substances and the process had strangely not been one of self-effort. The Big Book describes AA's common miracle like this: *"We will see that our new attitude toward liquor has been given us without any thought or effort on our part. It just comes! That's the miracle of it. We are not fighting it, neither are we avoiding temptation. We feel as though we have been placed in a position of neutrality- safe and protected. We have not even sworn off. Instead, the problem has been removed. It does not exist for us."*[23] Millions of recovered alcoholics attest to the accuracy of this most profound statement without equivocation. This description of AA's "psychic change" is spot on. It is no theory. The description is my experience exactly.

Unfortunately for me, and I reckon others like me, the impact of God's miracles lose vitalness with the passage of time. Subconsciously credit for the miracle

---

[23] *Alcoholics Anonymous*, p. 85.

began to shift from God to me. After all, wasn't I now an AA guru so many looked to for whatever AA had to offer? Had I not gotten a sponsor, taken the Steps, attended the meetings of my home group faithfully? Had I not done the "footwork" when others passed on the opportunity? I began to handle being "a good person" without God's constant attention. God had more pressing concerns than the comparatively mild "drama" of my life in sobriety. I just came to need God less.

The thrill and faith that came from having God miraculously remove a desire to drink had faded into life, the very life I had wished for so impetuously in early sobriety. My picturesque circumstances slowly eased into a facade and projecting the facade replaced the freedom of brokenness. My spiritual life had deteriorated into a fearful struggle to act as though I had it all together, dispense vital pieces of spiritual insight to those around me, rationalizing poorly made decisions and, with all humility (tongue and cheek), to shine a light on my new "earned" righteousness. Like a pebble in my shoe, a nuisance of angst left me undefinably unsatisfied. "Working the steps" stopped working. There was no thought of drinking but otherwise I was spiritually stuck. It seemed the harder I tried the more stuck I became.

Relying on the "God of my understanding," which had been sufficient to bring about a psychic change and a spiritual awakening, began not to fill my God shaped hole. Good things became bad things as I started to use them for spiritual substitutes, my reputation as a "good person" being the primary example.

As I started to rely on self-effort to manage my life after addiction to alcohol, I developed a deceptive notion that the loving God I had decided to turned my will and life over to in Step 3, the one who had performed a miracle in me, began to demand self-effort. My reputation as having it "all together" supplanted the freedom of transparency. The diligence of reputation building has a way of taking on momentum. My freedom had been slowly eroding and the pace felt like it was quickening.

Figuring out God's will for me as seemingly insinuated in AA's eleventh step (praying only for knowledge of God's will) and muscling up the self discipline to execute in that general direction as apparently suggested in AA's twelfth step (practice these principles in all our affairs) consumed the better part of my spiritual thought-life. Time sober in AA without the Gospel, after the miracle's pink cloud trails away, is a slide toward chronic human assumption of control. Was the bad thing that just happened my will or God's? AA doctrine appeared to be that two tracks of choice ran through this journey of life: my will and God's will.

When the undesirable happened, due to a poor decision or by perceived happenstance, I concluded actions emanating from my ungodly, selfish will were to blame. The world revolved around me. My understanding of this loving God, that went unchallenged by the openendedness of the 12 Steps and the legalistic moorings of my childhood religion, began to offer up a lot of guilt. In self evaluation I showed much improvement. God had taken my desire to imbibe substances and I was busy cashing in on His blessings. Why wasn't that enough?

I wasn't very good at figuring out God's will and I had to hide the frustration or damage my reputation as an AA guru. Plagued by general discouragement and a gnawing feeling deep inside God was disappointed with the way I felt, my existence was evolving into a hard way to live. I wanted the pink cloud of early sobriety back. I assumed a successful career path would yield some sort of pink cloud and my priorities began to reflect this belief.

In troubled times, when guilty willingness struck, I prayed, "God, please, just show me what to do (your will) and I'll do it!" I was constantly trying to jump the tracks from my will back to God's. These efforts were my new bootstraps. Turns out pulling myself up by these new bootstraps worked no better in sobriety than the old ones had in addiction. Fueled by self-effort, jumping the tracks back into God's will was my cause *de jure*. I wasn't living the alcoholic lifestyle and that justified my secret feeling, "Thanks God, I'm sober, I deserve these blessings. Can I get a little more if my behavior improves?"

In good times, I might give God mock appreciation before inwardly, almost subconsciously, taking credit for my arrival back on the track of His will, or more accurately, what I thought was His will. After a while I just took credit, with and without subtlety. My emptiness demanded I receive credit for my righteous choice to choose God's will over my own. I became an expert at retracing the scenarios of my experience to identify God's inflection point in deciding to reward my righteousness and turn things my way, or vice versa. Mostly it was vice versa. My spiritual thought-life was centered around taking credit for the bad and giving God credit for the good. After seven years that began to seem unfair. I got tired of taking the blame for the bad stuff and denying the guilt I was accumulating.

The spiritual ebb and flow was entirely frustrating and the bewilderment over my inability to nail down God on His will for my life began to unwittingly pluck my faith. Why would God have a plan for my life, designed for me personally, and make it so hard to discern? It made no sense. Why was God hiding such valuable information from me? I was having little to no success breaking His code and I could feel it deep down.

In retrospect, I was contorting to avoid the bad and bring on the good. I was constantly trying to manipulate God with my "good" behavior. Though sobered by grace, I became a reflective legalist resigned to the mission of figuring out then solving life's problems best I could. Slowly God had assumed the role of keeping score and holding my scorecard. My relationship with God was like a daily visit from an anal retentive Santa Claus constantly checking his list.

Somehow I felt I was never going to discover, much less understand, my mission in this world. How could God be vital to my contentment when I was constantly trying to solve the torturous mystery of His will? While my insides churned my outsides continued to look pretty good so I muddled along. Deteriorating relationships provided some sense of urgency and spurred my search for an intellectually honest answer to my growing dilemma.

As life became more and more about manipulating God to get my righteous due (and the stuff that came with it) He grew distant without me having made a decision for that to happen. I found myself wearing a mask with the default life strategy of "fake it to you make it" in place and growing strong. I returned to being a "poser" and didn't even know it. With the passage of time it just happened. I thought eventually accumulating enough days sober would provide an answer. More sobriety was my answer and seemed to be AA's.

Such was my spiritual health when I stumbled across Sonship and something called "Christian apologetics." Christian apologetics is a doctrine, or theology, or way of interpreting Scripture, which gives the skeptic permission to use his noggin' to evaluate the Bible. Christian apologetics is a powerful use of logic to uncover the truth and majesty of Scripture all the while fully acknowledging faith as an essential element. For example, the Bible's weaving of the Old and New

Testament (Covenant theology) could hardly be the work of man when analyzed through the lens of Christian apologetics. The same can be said of Biblical paradox, which was a really, really important aspect of Christian apologetics to someone on post at my spiritual station.

    Christian apologetics is defined as a method of evaluating Christian doctrine which defends Christianity against objections. That's straight from the dictionary. "Apologetics" is from the Latin root word "apologia" which is defined as a formal written defense of one's opinion or conduct. The Greek word *"apologos"* means "a speech in defense." Famous modern day Christian apologist with whom you might be familiar include C.S. Lewis, G.K. Chesterton and R.C. Sproul. The Apostle Paul was one of the first and certainly the most gifted Christian apologist. This book, among other things, is an apologetic work defending the proposition that Alcoholics Anonymous is a construct of Biblical Reformed theology.

    The Bible and AA agree faith is required for spiritual understanding and they both agree that faith is by no means to be used to swallow perceived inconsistencies without question when experience doesn't match what is written. The Big Book makes its own brilliant apologetic defense of faith in God. The fourth chapter is an entirely apologetic work entitled *"We Agnostics."* The chapter avers, *"deep down in every man, woman and child, is the fundamental idea of God.*"[24] It uses electricity as an example of the unseen being reality and stressing that visual proof is science's weakest form of proof. The chapter also candidly states, *"People of faith have a logical idea of what life is all about."*[25] The Big Book's chapter *"We Agnostics"* is an astute piece of apologetic work defending the existence of God in a rudimentary fashion designed to influence the intended audience.

    As ridiculous as it sounds now, before Sonship I considered the first 164 pages of the Big Book of Alcoholics Anonymous much more profound than the entire Bible. What I had learned about God in AA came through profound experience. The Big Book's words were confirmed. The confirmation dwarfed what I had learned about God from the Bible. The virgin birth, the resurrection, Jesus' miracles, I professed to believe all that stuff. It was the safe play. I reasoned so much scholastic dynamism had been devoted to the Bible over the centuries there had to be more to it than I understood. "Church" would have died out long ago if those attending held the same level of interest as I did.

    I chalked up the church's longevity to an "opioid of the masses" thing; it's perpetuation powered by the emotions of society and society's need for an ethos to maintain order. On the other hand, there was no swaying

---

[24] Ibid, p. 55

[25] Ibid, p. 49

when it came to God as I grew to understand him in AA. At one point in my life I was under the complete control of addiction. Now my addiction to substances was gone and I knew there was no bootstrap I had pulled. I knew that. My apologetic chops rested on this incontrovertible foundation. I believed the invisible God was real to the marrow of my bones, or there 'bouts. If the Bible was to say anything cathartic to me an explanation of the first 164 pages of the book *Alcoholics Anonymous* had to be incorporated.

In comparison to the Big Book, the Bible seemed clunky. I perceived Scripture as a history of the rules and some fair advice with dire warnings mixed in for guilty measure. Reading Scripture was a yawn. *"For God so loved the world that he gave his only begotten son, that whosoever believeth in him shall not perish but have everlasting life."*[26] Everlasting life? What about the next week?

The Bible's one answer wasn't faith in Jesus as far as I could tell. The answer to every problem, the description of one's Christian duty, seemed to be the same- just try harder. Pray more, read the Bible more, go to church more, put your shoulder to the spiritual wheel, "get 'er done," just pull yourself up by your bootstraps and do right, was the message I got. God might be pleased momentarily if sufficient effort produced measurable

---

[26] John 3:16

results. It seemed the Bible promised the best, easiest lives to those who could master the art of delayed gratification. Such mastery centered on resisting temptation in order to act according to Christian "do"s and "don't"s. That's bad news to someone who had failed on countless missions to significantly delay gratification through self-discipline. On occasions of sincere regret I earnestly resolved to act according to what the Bible seemed to demand only to make the same self-destructive decisions at crunch time. In addiction I truly wanted to want to.

    At crunch time the Biblical path had no sparkle. Frankly, it didn't have much sparkle before crunch time either. The stiff-necked herd who preached the Bible's "good news" were some of the most boring people I knew. Say what you will about alcoholics but boring we're not. The people at this new church weren't as colorful as a bunch of recovering drunks but they did admit to being sinners, present tense. They weren't as real as the people in AA but they weren't fake either. They were real enough that I couldn't ignore their claims the Bible addressed my concerns about "next week" in a way opposite of "just try harder." Their confidence in my ignorance was impressive and held my attention.

    Explaining to church friends that I knew God was real because of what I experienced as the result of the 12 Steps drew blank stares. They had no answer or explanation for my psychic change as I described it to them. They just insisted there was more. I thought, "more?!" I have "more" than you. God delivered me from addiction. What's He done for you on that scale? Whenever doubt creeped in I could always know God was real because I had absolutely no desire to imbibe alcohol, none. I didn't see they had anything like that level of faith in their lives.

    I don't think these churchgoers believed my AA spiel but functionally it didn't matter. After all, I had stumbled on to their turf. God had not compelled them to seek me out. Nevertheless, I couldn't see they had quite as big a hook upon which to hang their faith. I wasn't completely wrong but far from right. It turns out the giant hook they have is the unmatched peace that comes through a growing faith in the Bible's promises. I was unaware the Gospel has legs passed anything to do with a code of conduct. Biblical sanctification was a hook about which I knew nothing. Not knowing what sanctification is while enveloped in AA's version of it is beyond confusing. (Much more on sanctification later). I was trying to find my way with half a map.

    In my defense, pure Biblical theology didn't look like much of a hook at the time. I treated the Gospel as a poker hand where the cards are shown at the moment of death. There was always the possibility the Bible was some cosmic bluff of ancient history. Earthly function of the Gospel in my life had been limited despite some of my best efforts. In my experience the Gospel might be true but it had not proven to hold the power of AA. The AA evidence was undeniable and the AA experience a rock of truth.

What Sonship was about to show me was a paradoxical path to some serious freedom Jesus style. Not knowing that one doesn't know is the most debilitating form of ignorance. I was grossly mistaken in my belief AA had turned me into a good person. A sober person, yes. A good person, upon honest inspection (an honest tenth step), no. Abandoning the belief God grades on a curve, for a sober alcoholic with no desire to drink and a new life, just messes up everything.

For me to be open to seeing something I didn't know I didn't know, the revelation had to withstand honest, intellectual pursuit. It's a good thing Reformed believers are natural apologist. The first hurdle of faith was Sonship's opening contention regarding the human heart. When the Sonship material suggested there were no "good" people at heart, that given the opportunity, we all act selfishly, at least in part, I was insulted. I was a sober, respected member of the community. The Bible's contention that at a heart level there are no "good" people, including me, was frankly disrespectful. The Bible's claim that there is Sin in everything I do was down right defamatory. I was quite miffed. Think I'm not a good person? You should have seen me in active addiction! Just because I'm not perfect doesn't mean I'm not "good."

This was my intuitive, gut-level reaction to what felt like an accusation. Considering all the people in jail, politicians, the billions of godless Chinese communist, the millions of vodka-drinking Russians and all my former drinking buddies, I had to be in God's top 10%. Comparatively speaking, I was pretty darn good. If heaven was real, and I suspected it was, God wasn't going to deny someone in "good's" top 10%. The way I understood heaven there was plenty of room.

Upon encouraged reflection I had to admit there was evil in this world. When pressed, I couldn't point out evil's border either. Unable to gin a counter argument, my friends took the opportunity to slip what the Bible asserted through the eye of my scrutiny's needle. Jesus said no one is "good."[27] Even the Apostle Paul said he wasn't "good." Confronted with the evidence I had to take the supposition on face value or profess disbelief in the Bible. Not ready to do that, I begrudgingly agreed to the hypothetical. I didn't like it. I'm sure my arrogant stupidity amuses God at times.

That small amount of surrender shined a light in a dark place of my understanding. A layer of the onion was pealed. What happened surpassed all my expectations. It was beyond my comprehension that making God a compromiser was a prison. I thought being liberated from

---

[27] Mark 10:18, *inter alia*

the legalistic God of my childhood propelled my spiritual journey in AA. I was wrong.

My new friends never anticipated Reformed theology would explain the power found in the 12 Steps, nor did I. The Bible's explanation of the 12 Steps is not empirical but specific. I am convinced my friends teaching Sonship expected Biblical Reformed doctrine to collide with AA doctrine and then for God's truth to win out. God's truth won out alright but no collision with AA doctrine ever happened.

I had been barking up the wrong tree trying to discern my will from God's. Had not God's will happened in my life yesterday? Or last week? Or last year? What had happened, good or bad, or in between, sure as heck wasn't my will. There could be no argument before that bar. To have permission to live life under the pretext that God's will happens and that I can go kicking and screaming or in humble submission, became a game-changer. (Hang in there. This is going to make sense with a little honest consideration.)

I had been raised to believe God's will for me was to strive to attain an ability to behave according to God's law. That was my job, my part in the *quid pro quo* with God. To the degree I could muster the will power to follow His law, hop the track from my will onto the track of His will, I would receive His blessings; a good job, a beautiful wife and wonderful children. In my case, since I love to play golf so much, if I was really good, a membership at a nice country club with a scratch handicap for good measure, was achievable. I could not conceive of another way to read the Bible outside the *quid pro quo* formula.

The theology I was missing might best be glimpsed in John 6:29, *"Then they inquired, "What must we do to perform the works of God?" Jesus replied, "The work of God is this: to believe in the One He has sent."* There's a show stopper. What about striving to be good little boys and girls, Jesus?

In my mind I was having acceptable success keeping the Ten Commandments in sobriety. I was really pretty good at it, just ask me. Though I couldn't recognize it at the time, I had become AA's version of a Pharisee. Deceived by the neatly enticing theology of "works righteousness," another name for the *quid pro quo,* I was making great strides in the obedience department. There were many economic and social rewards. Following a set of rules, in this case AA guru rules, which looked a lot like Biblical rules to me, to claim the prize of being declared righteous enough, had become what my spiritual life was about. In sobriety I found myself able to delay gratification as never before and the result was an admiration for the simplicity of the *quid pro quo*. It looked like I was winning it just didn't feel like it.

Sonship had my number. The first homework assignment is to pray for God to reveal your Sin (character defects) to you. Buckle your chinstrap before you send that one up. Sin is seen walking in the valley, not peering from a mountain top. On that first night our Sonship host warned the group about praying for valleys, even indirectly. I blew it off as some hocus pocus drama for which the overly religious seem to have an affinity. I should have been paying attention.

What I was about to be exposed to, a literal reading of the Bible, was amazing and meshed perfectly with the AA experience. I was misunderstanding the tenth, eleventh and twelfth steps of AA. Needless to say, I was shocked to experience a Reformed-theology-illuminated extrapolation of AA principles. There was another spiritual awakening out there. It is a sustaining spiritual awakening, which offers a path to spiritual maturity past pink clouds. For me, this Sonship food was seasoned to taste.

Chapter 6

The Paradoxical Power Of Faith

Question: Once a person becomes a Christian does that person become more or less sinful?

The Apostle Paul describes himself as the worst of sinners -present tense- as he wrote letters of the New Testament no less! (1 Timothy 1:15, "*Here is a trustworthy saying that deserves full acceptance: Christ Jesus came into the world to save sinners- of whom I <u>am</u> the worst.*") Paul also claimed to be able to justly and boldly go before the very throne of a just God without fear and apprehension. (Ephesians 3:12, "*In him and through faith in him we may approach God with freedom and confidence.*") How could the Apostle Paul logically have such confidence approaching a just God being the worst of sinners? Why is it such a big deal that he could?

The short answer, in Church words, is that Paul was no longer under the law due to the imputed righteousness afforded by his faith in Christ, not his personal "works." Paul's righteousness came through faith not law-keeping. Those are some good sounding Church words with cataclysmic implications. I was completely oblivious. I was unaware of what the disease concept of Alcoholics Anonymous had really done for me. **The paradoxical power that comes from righteousness by faith, the power that comes from being out from**

under God's law, is the mightiest available to a human being.

Once the faith from my AA spiritual awakening began to go stale I needed "more." I was ready for more but under the one enormous, non negotiable condition mentioned earlier. The only way I could be given "more" was if "more" came aligned with the principles I witnessed producing miracles day in, day out, in the rooms of Alcoholics Anonymous. After all, I am one of those miracles. I knew beyond any doubt my sobriety had come from Almighty God, my Creator, as I experienced Him taking the 12 Steps in the program of AA.

The prospect that "more" could and would come from the Bible wasn't a far-fetched proposition. The hitch in that giddy up was that I thought I knew what was written in Bible. In reality I had no clue. The cultural Christianity of my youth had left me barren. Consequently, I had never considered the significance of foundational Biblical doctrines or how they applied to my personal experience with the 12 Steps of AA.

Two of the many Biblical doctrines beyond my understanding were the doctrines of "justification" and the aforementioned "imputed righteousness." I had no idea how essential an understanding of these doctrines are to explaining AA's success sobering drunks.

According to the Bible the point a person puts their faith in Jesus, acknowledging He is the Son of God and that He died and rose again "to save us from our sins" is referred to as "justification." Justification is a point in time. "Imputed righteousness" is the doctrine stating that Jesus' perfect record of righteousness is transposed onto the believer at the time of justification. My childhood experience in the church was filled with references and half descriptions of these doctrines. I had seen the "Jesus Saves" bumper stickers. There was nothing new here until what the Bible said about the purpose of God's law (Ten Commandments) happened to get explained.

For God to be a righteous, glorious, just God, His judgment must be fair. The doctrine of "imputed righteousness" allows God to reward the sinner eternal nirvana in heaven and remain a just God. In the respect that God looks at the justified sinner and sees Jesus' sinless record, the answer to our "trick question" is, of course, the new Christian becomes less sinful, infinitely less sinful. I can't remember not knowing this answer to the "trick" question.

There is, however, another Biblical perspective critical to understanding the Good News and how it ignites the potency of faith. It lies in the alternative answer to the trick question. It lies in the Biblical principle that maturing spiritually requires using God's law to grow an awareness of sin. In the seventh chapter of Romans Paul uses the sin of "coveting" to explain this principle of tectonic importance. AA uses this Biblical principle of tectonic importance to great effect.

The Tenth Commandment's prohibition on coveting is very unique. All the other Ten Commandments address either our relationship with God or our relations with others. The sin of coveting another's property, a victimless crime so to speak, is used by Paul to illustrate the proper use of God's law. Using God's law as a mirror is the only way we can healthfully and honestly examine our Sin to discover sinful motives.

Paul writes in Romans that had not the Commandment prohibited coveting he would not have known coveting is sinful. Paul reasons he therefore would not be accountable to God for this sin absent the law. A just God cannot hold us to account for committing sin we do not know is sin. With God, ignorance of the law is an excuse. **From this perspective, Paul points out God's law creates sin and that is a big, huge deal.**

Romans 5:20 is clear, *"The purpose of the law was that sin might increase."* I doubt those who display the Ten Commandments over the cash register or in their front yards understand. I wonder how many churchgoers who claim to love God's law know it was created so that sin would increase. According to the Bible, God's law is certainly worthy of adoration but not because it can produce any righteousness that will improve our standing with God. Paul says in Galatians, 3:10, *"all who rely on observing the law are under a curse."* Galatians 3:25, *"Now that faith has come, we are no longer under the supervision of the law."* In all the Sundays of my youth I cannot recall hearing a single sermon preached on this principle of Scripture. I missed that Sunday too.

Notice Paul doesn't say the law is no longer pertinent or altered by the appearance of the long-prophesied Messiah. In the Sermon on the Mount, Jesus' explains He did not come to abolish the law, not one "jot or tittle" of it.[28] In fact, Jesus goes further. He says you know murder is breaking a commandment but so is being angry with your brother or sister. Jesus said if you look at a married person with a lustful notion you have committed adultery. You know lying is wrong but breaking your oath is just as bad. Jesus said love your enemy. He said be perfect as your Father in heaven is perfect.

The Bible also unyieldingly proclaims God's standard of justice. God doesn't grade on the curve. Deuteronomy 27:26, *"Cursed is everyone who does not continue to do everything written in the Book of the Law."* If the Bible is true any human judged by a just God without Jesus' legal standing is toast.

Why would a loving God make legal demands (the law) that are impossible to meet? Are these verses of Scripture not somehow contradictory? Are they not cruel? Is God's law really good since it was created that sin would increase? These questions are excellent apologetic

---

[28] Matthew 5

inquiries. The answers are truly majestic and faith building in the extreme.

The covenant message of the Bible is unique in the plethora of human religions. For those who have been imputed with the righteousness of Christ, God's law is not a code of conduct to be followed to achieve righteousness. In fact, the New Testament describes how just the opposite is true. Romans 7:5- *"For when we were in the realm of the flesh, the sinful passions <u>aroused by the law</u> were at work in us, so that we bore fruit for death."* Who knew the law aroused sinful passions? Becoming cognizant of how the law arouses "sinful passions" is a life changer.

Consider Romans 7:6, *"But now, by dying to what once bound us, we have been released from the law so that we serve in the new way of the Spirit, and not in the old way of the written code."* And Galatians 3:10, *"For all who rely on the works of the law are under a curse, as it is written: "Cursed is everyone who does not continue to do everything written in the Book of the Law."* In other words, God's law drives those who believe in the Bible and seek righteousness acceptable to God, in the direction of Jesus. Righteousness can come from nowhere else when the path of law-keeping is eliminated. Romans 10:4 says, *"Christ is the culmination of the law so that there may be righteousness for everyone who believes."* It doesn't say "for everyone who behaves." As we shall learn, any perceived success we have in keeping the law fueled by self effort creates arrogance and the misery that comes with it. Understanding this Scriptural truth is indispensable to grasping the profoundness of the alternative answer to the "trick" question. Our dependence on God grows when we get more sinful not less sinful.

When the rich young ruler came and asked Jesus what he needed to do to enter heaven Jesus said, "keep the law." The young man, not being very self aware, said, "I have." Jesus then said, "go sell everything you have and give it to the poor." The rich young ruler just walked away because he was wealthy and Jesus' suggestion was just a bridge too far.[29] In this way Jesus brings up our sins of omission. If you think you keep God's law sufficiently surely Jesus brought you to reality when he pointed out sins of omission. What a vast sea that is!

The law magnifies our character defects. The road to liberation is paved with dead notions a life of earthly contentment can be achieved by trying to keep the law. Attempting to realize a better relationship with God through following a bunch of rules, or laws, or "working" steps (as opposed to "taking" steps), whether studying the Bible or in AA, is a harsh existence. These efforts are but "filthy rags" (Isaiah 64:6) before the throne of God. Why? Because our motives, in whole or in part, are self-serving whenever we do anything. God is fully aware of our

---

[29] Matthew 19:16-30

secret thoughts. **A loving God would never make our ability to have a relationship with Him contingent on our ability to follow any laws or rules.**

God provides a spiritual solution no law-abiding or rule-keeping criteria can offer. The law is good because it acts as a mirror for the believer to see just how far short he falls of perfection. Used properly, and there is a trick to it, the law creates humility. God's law forces us to get honest about our motives on a heart level. The Bible says what it says. God's law is a motive mirror. Romans 3:20, *"Therefore no one will be declared righteous in His sight by observing the law; rather, through the law we become conscious of sin."* Magnified sin and awareness of our corrupt motives brings the believer closer to God. When Isaiah actually encountered God his immediate, involuntary response, *"get away from me Lord, for I am a sinful man"*[30] is quite revealing. When Jesus gave Peter a miracle fishing lesson he said the same thing.[31] Being close to God reveals sin.

Sin consciousness, and only Sin consciousness, brings the believer closer to God. Just ask any AA member who has experienced a spiritual awakening after taking the Steps. Desperate alcoholics come in the rooms of AA for a solution to a drinking problem. Thinking if they could just stop drinking everything would work itself

---

[30] Isaiah 6:5

[31] Luke 5:6

out, they have failed to consider alcoholic drinking is due to something besides lack of will power. They soon discover in Step 4 that drinking is only a symptom of their condition. To bring about the "spiritual awakening" described in Step 12, the first five steps of the AA program increase character defects. The AA tactic is the Biblical tactic. The Big Book just uses words that don't carry heaps of modern man-made prejudice and misunderstanding.

In the Bible, God's law, with its impossible demands, illustrates the magnitude of what Jesus did at the Cross. Comparing the requirements of God's law to our actual conduct, not to mention our thought-life, the intellectually honest must concede failure. This sounds an awful lot like bad news, but its not. Bear with me. The road to freedom as explained in the Bible is counterintuitive and full of mystical truth but rest assured it is starkly logical under close examination.

Remember the secret to life- gratitude. When we believe our sins past, present and future are forgiven even though we have done nothing to "earn" the forgiveness, gratitude and genuine humility happen. Any caveat, any hedge, any contingency based on our behavior, any contingency based on anything, regarding our forgiveness detracts from the ultimate gratitude and humility of coming to a meritless faith in God and His plan for salvation. Lasting liberation from guilt and shame comes only through faith in the proposition things have been squared away with God forever, period, the end. Faith that "Jesus Saves" is a minnow compared to the whale of "Jesus Has Saved."

That's the intuitive part. The seemingly illogical part, the part so hard to grasp, the part so easily forgotten, the part that is infinitely counterintuitive, is that liberation comes through faith. Logically, if the freedom of obedience (sobriety in the case of an alcoholic) doesn't come through obeying the law it has to come through something. That thing is faith. **That righteousness comes through faith is the hardest concept to internalize because the concept is so paradoxical and so adverse to our deepest understanding of nature.** The Gospel's grace sizzles the human brain's *quid pro quo* like nothing else. The human brain intuitively, involuntarily rest on the certainty of Sir Isaac Newton's Third Law of Motion- *for every action there is an equal and opposite reaction.* Newton proved mathematically what we witness in the physical world without fail- that forces come in pairs. Not so with God. God's scales don't balance. It makes the Gospel appear just too good to be true. Truly, it sizzles the mind.

That faith produces the humility to bring about obedience instead of self-effort has been referred to as "The Great Gamble of the Gospel." This "gamble" scares the peajeebers out of many legalistic Christian denominations and their keepers of doctrine. "Don't tell the flock they are not under the law! All forms of sin and licentiousness will breakout. They'll start lying, cheating, drinking, gambling, and having orgies. They will take license to engage in all kinds of depraved behavior! They'll take advantage of God's grace to sin like never before!"

Such is the attitude of those who think they are keeping the law sufficiently and/or fail to understand the depravity of their hidden heart motives. They know little to nothing about the power of humility and how it brings about obedience. They have never witnessed the behavior of one who has been relieved of the compulsion to drink after being awakened spiritually by the 12 Steps of Alcoholics Anonymous. The recovered alcoholic's radical change in behavior is the effects of gratitude and humility made easily observable. The behavior of those who have experienced a spiritual awaking as the result of AA's 12 Steps prove gratitude and humility do not produce sinful desires and licentiousness. Just the opposite.

In fact, the AA experience demonstrates compellingly that gratitude and humility are the only solution to the disobedience of habitual drunkenness. The AA methodology uses faith to produce gratitude and humility which results in sobriety for the alcoholic. Righteousness through faith produces the freedom of obedience in AA. People who underestimate or doubt the power of faith to bring about obedience need to witness what happens in the rooms of Alcoholics Anonymous.

Paul's letter to the Galatians amplifies the Gospel's message coopted by AA beautifully. In his letter to the Galatians, Paul finds the perfect opportunity to make his point that faith brings about humble obedience, not law-keeping. The letter must be history's most well received. The men of Galatia planned to get circumcised to make themselves part of Abraham's linage and therefore deserving heirs to everything Jesus offered. The Judaizers (Christian legalist) convinced the Galatians that just having faith wasn't enough. The Galatians' *quid pro quo* brains had them ready to endure a first century circumcision, a very painful affair to be sure; the *quid pro quo's* finest hour, so to speak.

At the time Christians were predominately Jewish. Jesus was Jewish. The blessing of Jesus as Messiah was a fulfillment of God's promise to Abraham, the first Jew. God had Abraham circumcise himself, his household and even his slaves. In the Old Testament Jews circumcised converts. In order to qualify to present Jesus' credentials before God's throne as their own, the Galatians reasoned becoming "Jewish" was in order and the act of circumcision was the ticket. They bought what the legalist were selling. The Galatians were seeking to make themselves "Jewish" by their own hand. They were seeking to make themselves more acceptable to God by their own hand. The Galatians were seeking to fulfill the requirements of God's law by their own hand.

The Galatians were ready to take great pride in their new faith by performing such an "impressionable" demonstration of their faith. "To be circumcised" or "be of the circumcision" would be something to brag about. Enduring such "private" pain would prove their faith. Who could doubt their level of commitment after a "weanie whacking?" Post op who could doubt their righteousness? They would have a sign of their righteousness to carry with them wherever they went for the rest of their lives. They would have a handy reminder of how they earned Jesus' atonement. The Galatians wouldn't need as much grace after having their "weanie whacked for Jesus." The Galatians were out to earn a big ole helping of righteousness.

Paul goes ballistic and let's the Galatians have it with both barrels. His words are filled with exasperation. In the third chapter of Galatians he goes off, *"The law curses all who practice it and fail to do it perfectly…" "Who has bewitched you? Did you receive the Spirit by following the law or by believing what you heard?"* Paul exclaims that should the Galatians go through with this "demonstration of faith" Jesus would be of no value to them. Galatians 5:1-2 *"It is for freedom that Christ has set us free. Stand firm then, and do not let yourselves be burdened again by a yoke of slavery. Mark my words! I, Paul, tell you that if you let yourselves be circumcised, Christ will be of no value to you at all."* Paul's message to the Galatians is plain and straight to the point. You can't fix yourselves. The "yoke of slavery" referenced is the yoke of being under the law. Paul says trying to fix yourselves is slavery.

The Bible says in many ways and in many places that staring into the mirror of God's law with the recognition of our powerlessness to abide by it, coupled with the understanding of God's demand for perfection, leaves no choice but unconditional surrender. Before learning about Reformed theology, I glanced into the law's mirror every now and again. I recognized some superficial failings. I just surmised the loving God who had delivered me from addiction to substances would never turn around and condemn me for not being perfect. **I was completely missing the point. I could not see that this attitude had me spiritually stuck. I could not see the walls of my "works righteousness" prison.** I had no idea I was passing on the ultimate freedom by making God a compromiser. By making God a compromiser I was making him a scorekeeper. There is no freedom in making Santa Claus your God. There is no freedom in trying to get God to like you better, or just enough.

The Big Book provides a very tangible illustration of the truth that sinners have better "ears" than the "righteous." In the chapter "To The Wives," four descriptions of an alcoholic are listed. Each alcoholic is in greater despair than the last. Each one has less "righteousness" than the one before. The Big Book points out the alcoholic who has lost everything, the one caught in the cycle of hospitals and sanitariums, is the alcoholic most easily reached.

It's common knowledge an alcoholic must "hit bottom" before help will help. Why an alcoholic must hit bottom is a mystery to those who do not understand the nature of the problem. A "bottom" is just a secular term for a "complete loss of righteousness." An alcoholic's bottom, the point at which a spiritual solution requiring surrender will be considered, is nothing more than a sufficient loss of righteousness at any point in time. The condition in AA is termed "spiritual bankruptcy."

"Sober" in AA connotes a state of being free from the desire to drink, not chemical abstinence. Legions come to AA in order to stop drinking. Not having a sufficient loss of righteousness, they want to achieve sobriety and move on with their lives. Some come to complete surrender, some don't. God's criteria in AA is no different than anywhere else. It's the whole enchilada or nothing.

Those that choose to keep on fighting attempt to "use" the Steps to achieve their ends. It never works. The surrender is not there. Some twisted need for righteousness, some clamp of Adam's genetics, has them still maneuvering to outflank addiction. They just can't start getting more "sinful" past their drinking or using. Mistakenly, they consider their addiction responsible for their lying, cheating and stealing lifestyle or their "need-to-keep-secrets" lifestyle. Take the addiction away and the lying, cheating and stealing will go with it they reason. It's a hardy lie disguised in the cloak of "works righteousness." They are blinded by the perception one has the ability to earn sobriety using the Steps.

Being blinded by the "earned righteousness" lie is hardly limited to alcoholics seeking sobriety. All sons and daughters of Adam stumble around in the darkness of addiction to their preferred substitute for God. The AA process and the Gospel rest on the same great paradox- the healing of humility and gratitude comes when sin gets bigger in the estimation of the sinner, not smaller. Humility and gratitude grow with a growing dependence on God.

Chapter Seven

The Real Deal Of Righteousness

The Pharisees, Sadducees and the scribes, collectively the Pharisees for our purposes, were the religious leaders of Judaism in Jesus' day. The spiritual outlook of a Pharisee is characterized by **a *low view of sin***. A low view of sin focuses on acts, not corrupt motives and selfish attitudes. Being able to recognize a "low view of sin" is important because a "low view of sin" produces "**cheap grace**." Freedom is fleeting carrying around "cheap grace." The Pharisees were custom-made for illustrating the prison constructed by a "low view of sin" and the "cheap grace" that comes with it.

The Pharisees were the only group condemned by Jesus and, boy, did he know how to push their buttons. These men, steeped in the law since early childhood, loved the Scriptures as a code of conduct. They were all about perfecting the illusion of having the will power and desire to act righteously. They took great pride in the holiness and piety that came with their solution to the Sin problem- try hard to obey the law. Walking around with their noses in the air, "surrender" was a foreign concept, a path completely closed to them. In their mind's eye they were not genetically capable of spiritual bankruptcy. Spiritual surrender was not in their DNA.

The Pharisees earned Jesus' distain because they were incapable of loving anyone but themselves. They claimed to be without sin and perfect keepers of the law by virtue of their conduct, their sacrifices at the Temple and the very fact they were Jewish. Their righteousness came from law-abiding, their Jewish linage and their reputation. As minsters of the law, "developers" of doctrine as it were, their self-righteousness spilled over into demands others follow "God's law" as they wrote and interpreted it. By coming up with extensions of God's law they yoked the Jews of Jesus' day in the name of pointless piety. They cared nothing for the people. The Pharisees had no sympathy for those who wore their yoke. To gain glory for themselves and muster a respect for their righteousness was the heart-level motivation. Cluelessly convinced God sanctioned their attitudes, the Pharisees' spiritual pursuits were focused on squashing any doubts about their personal righteousness. The Pharisees were human voids of humility. They manufactured darkness and found morbid satisfaction in their vocation.

The commandment to keep the Sabbath day holy offered the Pharisees a favorite opportunity to add to the law. Decreeing all kinds of practices as prohibited on the Sabbath is a good example of their depravity. It was easy to expand the rules for the Sabbath. The Pharisees considered making new rules for the Sabbath an opportunity to design a path to "spiritual growth" for their followers. Their rules were meticulous and attempted to cover any contingency. Their obsession with works righteousness was insane. These idiots were after Jesus for healing the sick and crippled on the Sabbath.

The Pharisees, all of whom were wealthy, demanded esteem due to their wealth, their alleged intellectual prowess as exhibited by their knowledge of the law and their publicly displayed will power to obey it. They reasoned their wealth and social standing was proof-positive God liked them better than just regular folks. With this arrogance they meted out punishment for violations of their ever-expanding legal requirements with self-righteous, thinly disguised glee. The Apostle Paul started out as one of these characters and details "the delight of the Pharisee" in Scripture.[32] Their whole self-worth was wrapped up in their conviction God needed and appreciated their help. The Pharisees, so proud of their good character, were completely unaware that exalting themselves as examples of how to live while sitting in judgment of others robbed them of joy and the ability to love. Jesus called them a den of vipers and described their spiritual conditions as white-washed tombs.[33] Ouch!

The Pharisees were too arrogant to comprehend the Gospel's message that righteousness comes by faith

---

[32] Philippians 3:5

[33] Matthew 23:7

and faith alone. Those found to be lacking in "law-keeping righteousness" owed sacrifices to the Temple in proportion to their sin. The practice was a cash cow similar to the Church's practices of selling indulgences during the time of Martin Luther. Any doctrine that righteousness comes through faith and through faith only, threatened their wealth and their self image as being "good" people. Some dude walking around performing miracles proclaiming righteousness comes only by faith was a crisis of the greatest magnitude.

The miracle-working Jesus turned the ancient political and economic power structure of Jerusalem upside down with this one singular doctrine- that righteousness comes through faith, not works. The doctrine has been toppling political and economic power structures ever since. The Gospel's message has not lost any measure of potency in the thousands of years since God made His promise to Abraham. When Abraham showed the faith to slay his only son Isaac, Abraham's faith was "credited to him as righteousness" by God.[34] This was long before God gave his law to Moses. The doctrine of righteousness through faith has stood the test of time as has no other theology in the history of mankind.

Jesus taught that "believers" who consider themselves capable of pure motives and/or believe "God

---

[34] Genesis 15:6

helps those who help themselves" live imprisoned by the bars of arrogance. The mirror of God's law is foggy and yields a "low view of sin" for "good people" dealing with a compromising God. They just aren't forced to rely on God as much as the hopeless sinner.

The crowds who heard this outrageous message of righteousness through faith and faith alone were no less astonished and bewildered than the Pharisees. Only the miracles of Jesus, His subsequent willingness to be crucified and raised from the dead, gave Him the massive "street cred" required to challenge the worldly logic of "works righteousness." That obeying God's law, or making an acceptable attempt, earns an easier life with less suffering, then heaven at death, was the *quid pro quo* theology of the Pharisees. The inclination to believe the *quid pro quo* is so strong no half measures by God to contradict it would do. The *quid pro quo* of the Pharisees' theology is logical stuff to the intellect of men, as easy a sell today as it was then. To the postmodern world dominated by man's esteem for man's wisdom, the Gospel's lunacy stands undiminished.

The logic of *quid pro quo* theology is in the DNA of all the world's religions except one. Biblical Christianity's denial of "works righteousness" in favor of the righteousness by faith doctrine is the most profound distinction of religious doctrine philosophically available. No doctrinal difference could be more contentious than righteousness by faith, none. All religions are about righteousness and how to get it. Doing the right actions to achieve a wonderful life and afterlife is the game played and the game coached. With the single exception of Biblical Christianity, human religions are about what to practice so that death brings a good result after a satisfying life. Christianity is about what to **believe** so that death brings the desirable result after a satisfying life.

Christianity is about what to believe in order to transcend suffering with humble joy. For the person willing to bite on the proposition righteousness comes through faith, the test of the doctrine's validity becomes a matter of honesty regarding one's motives. Can we be honest enough to recognize the pervasiveness of our self-serving motives? Is the honesty, or desire, or whatever it takes, there to consider that every good thing we've ever done had an ulterior motive? Can Sin be seen as so pervasive as to leave one hopeless? The realization one is hopeless to keep God's law sufficiently is completely analogous to how the disease concept leaves the alcoholic hopeless.

The proof of what Jesus taught is in the pudding. The freedom that comes in the thought-life (spiritual condition) of those liberated from the burdens of the law is real. The sobriety in AA is obedience that comes *"without any thought or effort on our part."*[35]

---

[35] *Alcoholics Anonymous*, p. 85

Righteousness in AA comes through humility produced by faith not arrogant law-keeping. AA proves Jesus right.

How much Pharisee can you see in yourself? It's in there. Even the most ardent believers in righteousness by faith have the *quid pro quo* DNA lurking amongst the molecules of their theological genes. An instinctive need for justification by "works righteousness" is a good way to summarize the condition of Sin that comes from Adam.

"Righteousness by works" is the deepest part of our sin nature. I'm a good person. I'm sober. I go to meetings. I go to church. I am a hard worker. I give to charity. I'm better than that person. I'm worse than that person. I do this. I do that. I'm this way, not that way. My intentions are good. These characteristics may be an accurate description on some level but without evaluating the motives behind our actions and attitudes, these outward pieces of evidence mean nothing. They offer no evaluation of the heart. Jesus dealt with issues of the heart. Jesus was about healing our hearts. Only a healed heart can transcend earthly suffering.

Deep down we humans seek to put God in our debt, or worse yet, be our own God. We need to deserve less suffering. That "God will owe me" or "God will like me more" constantly finds its way into our psyche somehow, even the psyche of those who ascribe to the truth that righteousness comes through faith. The *quid pro quo* theology is the believer's crafty, villainous, resilient menace. Unrecognized it allows a perceived "good work," however well intentioned, to temporarily quench our thirst for earned righteousness and steal the freedom that comes from the humility of God's grace.

The *quid pro quo* theology's kryptonite is grace. The self-conclusion "I'm deserving" or "I'm a good person" battles with grace for the square footage of our souls. One overtakes the other as light grays out dark. Whether in the form of the slightest unconscious thought or a full throated demand for perceived righteousness due, the sinister *quid pro quo* is there to thwart our ability to completely accept God's grace. Pride steals freedom.

Deriving our self-worth based on our deeds, or more likely our misdeeds, makes looking into the mirror of God's law too demoralizing for the unbeliever and the legalist. Without the unearned forgiveness of the cross, God's mirror of the law reflects a shame and guilt not freedom. A compromising God puts the freedom that comes with deep introspection out of reach. Honestly look into God's law without Jesus' imputed righteousness and you'll need a stiff drink.

Only the mirror of the law coupled with an unassailable forgiveness can subdue the pervasiveness of the *quid pro quo* poison in our thought-life. Seeing, then admitting our shortcomings and humbly accepting Jesus' forgiveness marks the path to discovering our way out from the dark prisons of the *quid pro quo* and the slavery of spiritual self-sufficiency. The prison of "works righteousness" has heavy doors unlocked by the key of humility. The lock has no other key.

The hard thing about explaining this has to do with context. How can figuring out my motives are selfish help my self esteem? Great question. Is the "righteousness by faith" way of life a self-condemning exercise without end? Sounds like it doesn't it? Taken in the context of life before surrendering to God the constant examination of motives would be self-condemning and terribly damaging to one's self-esteem, *ad infinitum*. Confidence everything is squared away with God is essential to avoiding an unhealthy, torturous focus on our sin.

The Gospel and AA allow our faith to define us in a very special way. Paradoxically, the freedom of obedience comes when being perceived as obedient just doesn't matter that much any more. It's a crazy thing. Humility is a different creature than what one might reason, or expect. It is the humility that makes the process of looking into the law a builder of self-esteem. There is no endless exercise of self-condemning reflection. Romans 8 says, *"Therefore, there is no condemnation of those who are in Christ Jesus."* The "therefore" refers to Paul's reasoning and assurances expressed in Romans 7. Those sobered in AA know full well the value of leaving off the condemnation.

Chapter 8
Making The Invisible Visible

The road to freedom is obscured and made rocky by our love of certain illusions. Holding the opinion that we are becoming less and less sinful, or are less sinful than we were, sucks us back under the law. The Pharisee in us does not go down without a fight. In the right context, awareness of our Sin produces a thought-life that sends messages of contentment. In the wrong context Sin awareness begets pure guilt and shame. It's a mysterious spiritual principle to be sure. Nevertheless this is precisely the case.

If spiritual growth was a process of getting less sinful spiritual growth would be marked by becoming less reliant on God. That makes no sense. The trick to spiritual growth is seeing "Sin." Spotting "sin" is easy; spotting "Sin" not so easy. When we become aware of how our incessant approval-sucking, our posing for the sake of reputation, our constant pursuit of the comforts that come with material things, our constant attempts to be our own God, or manipulate God, our slavery becomes apparent. Enslaved we get willing to "have God remove our shortcomings." AA proves it.

By coming to terms with our hidden self-seeking motivations our clandestine efforts to fix ourselves come out of hiding. Understanding how these never-before-detected motivations operate in our lives is spiritual growth. It takes willingness, practice, understanding confidants, Scripture and prayer.

Our faith and greater faith is blocked by the incessant, almost subliminal, inter voice urging us to submit to the notion something outside us will fix the inside of us. This inter voice blocks discovery of hidden motives. The yearning to find something outside of us that will fix the inside of us is our default mission in life. Fixing ourselves just feels like the responsible thing we should be doing.

The 12 Steps provide a perfect picture, a microcosm if you will, of how faith works to fill our emptiness and bring about some humble freedom. A person desperate enough to darken the doors of AA is not lacking in guilt or shame. Fear of the feelings produced by guilt and shame propel the alcoholic mind. The painful emptiness and suffering that are part and parcel of addiction act as the price of admission to AA. No one sitting in their first AA meeting is having a wonderful day. The motive for first meeting attendance is relief from severe emotional pain. Nobody tries AA first. No one gleefully picks AA.

Alcoholics are reduced to the primary coping mechanism of relying on the release offered by the effects of alcohol. For the alcoholic, the effects of alcohol fill up the God-shaped hole quite nicely and most reliably. Of course, the escapades of alcoholic drinking just beget more shame, more guilt, more fear and a more urgent need for more alcohol. The cycle of addiction is surely one of the most vicious in the human experience and it leaves the false but rational impression that alcohol is the problem.

Alcoholics Anonymous can show the alcoholic how this cycle of addiction is broken but only when the alcoholic is ready to surrender. Desperation produced by suffering is the essential element to the AA program of recovery. AA has no solution for anyone unwilling to admit powerlessness over alcohol and an unwillingness to accept the proposition there is an intelligent power in the universe greater than a human's. At its philosophical core, AA is about taking steps to channel desperation into faith.

In a most generic evaluation, the 12 Steps break the cycle of addiction by using desperation to infuse faith in the suffer's thought-life. Admittedly there is some subterfuge involved. The first element of faith in recovery is that taking the Steps can somehow elevate the compulsion to imbibe alcohol. The second level of faith, and the one proven to be most essential, is for the alcoholic to have just a willingness to believe in God. AA has proven such a willingness is sufficient to make a start if surrender has happened. For the Steps to channel desperation into a spiritual awakening there must be enough desperation for the alcoholic to be willing on a guttural level to accept the supposition that only a power greater than human power can deal with addiction. Some get desperate enough, some don't. Some get the willingness, some don't. AA can't provide these essentials. No one can. These essentials come from the God department.

The AA newcomer is exposed to "a power greater than ourselves" in Step 2. Right away "a power greater than ourselves" turns into "God as we understand Him" in Step 3. By Step 5, the person in recovery has moved into action and "God" is God. Action in the fifth step requires a faith in God big enough to admit to "God, ourselves and another human being the exact nature of our wrongs." By Step 7 the step-taker believes God is so large He can remove "shortcomings." These facts demonstrate inarguably that taking the 12 Steps of Alcoholics Anonymous is a Biblical "righteousness by faith" journey. The road to recovery in AA is a growing faith and a growing reliance upon God. The AA program is not one of becoming more and more obedient. It is not a process of developing will power.

The inventory of Step 4 and confession in Step 5 are pivotal. Every step-taker learns in Step 4 his character defects are far more expansive than first thought. The realization that the problem is not in the bottle but in the mirror comes hard to some but it must come if recovery is to take hold. **The AA methodology uses the word "inventory" in the fourth step to mimic the law's function as a mirror.** The word "inventory" in Step 4 is a very, very clever word in context and certainly evidence of the AA genus.

The first real action in the recovery process happens when the "fearless and thorough" moral inventory of Step 4 is shared with another person in Step 5. To unmask one's self in Steps 4 and 5 is the first "action" leap of faith and its significance cannot be overstated. Armies of alcoholics cycle through the rooms of AA pretending to have taken the first three steps. They're called "third steppers" by the AA old timers and sooner or later, without exception, these people suffer "dry drunks" (being irritable, restless and discontented to the extreme), drink again, or commit suicide.

The Big Book's statement regarding how seminal an event the taking of Step 5 can be is shocking. In effect, the text says exercising the faith to tell someone about all your garbage, leaving out nothing, predictably leads to a significant spiritual experience, a great feeling of closeness to God. *"The feeling that the drink problem has disappeared will often come strongly."*[36] The Big Book puts its credibility on the line here at Step 5, and justifiable so as it turns out. The experience of millions of recovered alcoholics affirm the claim. The Big Book's fifth step claim comes from experience, not theory or speculation.

The Big Book says Step 5 is the gateway to freedom and instructs those who would recover to take great care at this juncture of their recovery process. The text points out if the faith to take a complete fifth step is

---

[36] Ibid, p. 75

not present, if the person cannot take off their mask completely (or to the best of his ability at the time), chances of a successful recovery plummet.

    Most of us know the relief of confessing a corrosive secret. "The truth will set you free" is an axiom of known value. In many cases, the alcoholic seeking to recover doesn't understand how confessing "character defects" in an unmasking to another person has anything to do with being rid of a compulsion to enjoy the effects of alcohol. Truth be told, no one completely understands how Step 5 evokes the mysterious power of God so predictably. Growing one's "character defects" in Step 4 and Step 5's unloading of deepest secrets is an exercise of faith which has a sum greater than its parts. Experience has shown the first five steps of AA, the process of growing character defects only to confess them, can leave the alcoholic bathed in a new faith in God.

    There is an interesting "fifth step phenomenon" observable in the experience of AA which speaks to the "righteousness by faith" doctrine specifically. The faith to undertake this unmasking of newly realized "character defects" becomes an identifiable metric when subsequent fifth steps taken by those who relapsed into active addiction are examined. Once an initial leap of faith is used to overcome the giant hurdle of making one's self vulnerable in a first fifth step, the occurrence of "*a strong feeling the drink problem has been solved"*[37] seems to get used up.

Once faith is plied to the first unmasking and the unmasking occurs, the AA experience shows subsequent unmaskings are not as poignant as the first. One can logically understand the second decision to be unmasked doesn't require as much faith as the first. I am not aware of any sudden fifth step spiritual experiences as described on page 75 of the Big Book happening during a second unmasking when the first unmasking was earnestly undertaken. A reasonable deduction is that the faith to overcome the fear of unmasking is more vital to a spiritual awakening than the unmasking itself.

The undeniable difference in the levels of faith needed in a first fifth step and doing a second fifth step isolates the metric of faith. The greater faith in the first fifth step is obviously what provides the greater result. This observation is a glimpse into the mystery of righteousness by faith. The apologetic significance of analyzing faith as associated with AA's fifth step in regards to how righteousness by faith, and faith alone, brings about freedom is real.

The spiritual properties of being vulnerable in a properly done fifth step is the perfect picture of faith resulting in humility. Faith to grow your character defects in Step 4 and disclose them in Step 5 is the essential

---

[37] Ibid, p. 75

element to realizing the desired result- the willingness and the humility to undertake Step 6 and Step 7.

As mentioned earlier, every other religion on earth has at its foundation a "works righteousness" ethos. The pioneers of AA cleverly designed the AA program around "steps," not laws or rules. They also "doubled down" on the concept of "righteousness by faith alone" by making it clear the AA program is a "suggestion" for those wishing to recover from addiction. The sentence before the steps in the text is: *"Here are the steps which are suggested (*emphasis added*) as a program of recovery:"*[38] AA is not "righteousness by working steps." If the Steps were "laws" or "rules" instead of "suggestions" they could not be rooted in the unique Christian doctrine of righteousness by faith. Again, the genus of AA and the 12 Steps shows through as Biblical righteousness by faith at its core.

Those that preach "just try harder" and self-help gurus sell the development of certain practices-of-the-human-will doctrine. Do this or that, think this or that, and your results (righteousness) will improve. No matter the flavor, at the end of the day, it's adhering to a code of conduct. While the follow-a-code-of-conduct theology can produce desirable economic, physical or relational results, no practice other than the discerning of one's own

---

[38] Ibid, p. 58

corrupt motives can bring about a scintilla of Godly humility.

If AA doctrine contradicted the doctrine of "righteousness by faith," AA would be no commentary on Reformed theology and Reformed theology would have nothing to say to alcoholics recovered or recovering in AA. A truncation of the 12 Steps is common in AA: "Trust God, clean house and help others." In church words: "have faith, confess/repent, witness." There is no "keep-the-law" in either. AA's 12 Steps and the Gospel are perfectly aligned in this most distinguishing characteristic of practice and thought. The symmetry is enthralling and certainly no coincidence!

Being declared righteous by just believing is an amazing concept only the most loving God could offer. No path to freedom could be more widely available. No distinguishing intellect or manufactured constitution of will is required. The believer's challenge, or quest, is to acclimate the reality sins have been forgiven into our day to day, minute to minute thought-life.

Sounds easy doesn't it?

Chapter 9

The Puzzle of Pride

Acclimating the doctrine that righteousness comes through faith into our thought-life is the hardest challenge for the believer. It's hard because humility is so paradoxical and the desire to be humble is so contrary to human nature. To understand how righteousness comes through faith an understanding of humility is required.

AA's Step 7 is "humbly ask God to remove our shortcomings." A "peace that surpasses all understanding" comes when righteousness by faith gifts us with humility. If "righteousness by faith" produces humility and God's grace uses humility to produce obedience (sobriety), and obedience gives us the freedom we crave, then humility is the ticket!

The first part of the humility puzzle is its desirability. The primary block to enjoying humility is the acceptance that humility is the most gratifying emotional state enjoyed by humans. Our Adam DNA tells us humility is not the most gratifying emotional state enjoyed by humans. The world bombards us with the reinforcing messages that humility is not the ticket.

The second hurdle to claiming our "humility ticket" is understanding the nature of humility and how humans get it. Humans cannot produce humility in themselves. Humility comes by being aware of one's arrogance which requires humility. The paradox is surely circular but examining the nature of humility will show us how God solves the conundrum.

Don't agree one can't conjure or manufacture humility? Think of the counterfactual statement of, "yes I can produce humility in myself." The statement is one of blatant, self-reliant arrogance.

Other religions on earth, and even legalistic Christians, would vehemently disagree with the supposition humility is not achievable by human effort. These religions would claim their theology produces the most humble practitioners, proving the legitimacy and supremacy of their theology's doctrine. An allegedly humble group claiming any accentuating superlative, particularly that of "most humble," is oxymoronic. Forgive the gratuitous observation.

Reformed Christians, taking que from the Apostle Paul's rumination of being "chief of sinners," would humbly consider themselves the most arrogant followers on the planet. Reformed Christianity stands alone in this regard. The two approaches, or the two sides of the argument, that we can or cannot produce humility in ourselves, are mutually exclusive. Both can't be right. AA theology aligns with one or the other.

Do you consider yourself a humble person? Do you consider yourself as possessing an acceptable level of humility? Truly humble people can't think themselves to be humble. One who correctly determines themselves the possessor of humility, or an ability to create it, would also

The Puzzle Of Pride

be the possessor of justified pride and/or arrogance. Prideful is the opposite of humble. Arrogance is the opposite of humility. One who correctly or incorrectly determines themselves to have humility, self-produced or not, possesses a proportional pride. This is sound logic. Arrogance can't create its opposite- humility.

There is a useful illustration of true humility in the HBO series *Band of Brothers* which is the true story of Easy Company, an outfit of American soldiers deployed in Europe during World War II. Captain Spears is describing to First Sargent Lipton a particular soldier who has held Easy Company together in the toughest, most harrowing times these combat veterans have endured. Spears then asks Lipton if he knows the soldier he is describing. Staring at Lipton, Spears muses, "you have no idea who I'm talking about do you?" Lipton responds with a blank, clueless expression to mumble, "no, sir." Spears then informs Lipton, "It's you First Sargent Lipton." The dialogue is a poignant illustration of true humility. Sargent Lipton couldn't have intentionally created something he did not know he had.

If one accepts the premise humans can't produce humility in themselves then one must accept humility is unearned. This acceptance makes "righteousness by faith" worth investigating because, if true, we have an answer to the conundrum. If we get humility through grace we have not earned it and therefore attaining it produces no pride within us. Others see growing humility in us before we realize something is bringing peace to our thought-life.

These understandings raise legitimate questions though. How can the supposition that righteousness comes from faith profoundly and uniquely alter a human's daily thought-life? What does it feel like on the inside? How does unearned humility grow us spiritually? These are profound questions. We can see that understanding "how humility actually works" is valuable, life-changing stuff.

According to the Bible, the ingrained law-keeping and the reputation-building demanded by the sin nature is opposite from the nature of "living in the righteousness provided by faith." Law-keeping and reputation-building repel humility because they are the product of human ingenuity. Law-keeping and reputation-building exercises build our "arrogance muscles." Our righteousness comes from "works" not "faith" when we seek to build our self-esteem using these tools.

God offers a different path to self-esteem. Seeing and feeling God's grace when looking at our pile of character defects is the happy, humble self-esteem that rest on the unshakable foundation of who God is, not who we are. God is trustworthy. We aren't. Operating with a thought-life controlled by works righteousness leaves our freedom in the hands of our fallible selves. Righteousness by faith leaves our freedom

The Puzzle Of Pride

in the hands of God and our ability to believe in His grace.

Believin' ain't easy though. The condition of our *quid pro quo* brains makes accepting grace irrational in our core. Turning from the "*quid pro quo*," is contrary to the deepest nature of humans. Through the ages humans have inflicted pain on themselves, made sacrifices on the alters of innumerable gods, including human sacrifices, and performed all manner of stupidity to appease the *quid pro quo* urge that dominates us.

Having faith an unseen God has chosen to give us righteousness we do not deserve is the most illusive faith of all. Again, the scales just don't balance. Our *quid pro quo* brains, our grace-ignorant brains, demand scales that balance. We get righteousness just by believing our sin problem has been dealt with by Jesus? Humility comes through just believing? Really? Pushing all the chips to the middle of the table on those cards is the hardest of all bets to make.

The Bible, however, is unequivocal. Trusting in Jesus' atonement for our sins is allowed. As the story goes, Jesus' atonement has paid the believer's sin debt to God in full. Jesus didn't just make a down payment. The Gospel declares having faith Jesus is exactly who he claims to be means we need not focus on our sin any longer. In fact, the Bible implores us to use faith to quit focusing on our Sin.

The *quid pro quo* forces us to focus on our Sin. The *quid pro quo* forces our thought-life into a constant calculation of how good or bad we are. A thought-life dominated by the *quid pro quo* is constantly evaluating life's circumstances to get an answer to this question and to map a course of action to get what we crave-righteousness. A thought-life dominated by the *quid pro quo* enslaves a human to the circumstances of life. Suffering cannot be transcended when our circumstances hold such a dominate influence.

Only God's grace can turn our focus away from our Sin. Not focusing on our Sin liberates our self-esteem from the works righteousness that focuses us on the messages coming from our circumstances. Ultimate freedom is when we can accept our "righteousness schemes" of law-keeping and reputation-building. When these schemes are accepted our humility brightens and our arrogance dims. There is another paradox at work. Becoming aware of our righteousness schemes diminishes their power to focus us on our circumstances. We get humility through this spiritual discernment regarding our motives. In this way the faith to rely on God's grace produces humility.

The notion we can do more about our Sin outside of repenting and making amends causes us to focus on it. The arrogant notion we have the power to purify our hearts leads to all kinds of misery. A "low view of Sin" produces scant humility. A "low view of Sin" requires only so much grace. A grace that leaves us responsible to earn any of God's favor is a "cheap grace." The arrogance of having a "low view of Sin" infects our thought-life with schemes to work for righteousness. If we could do anything about our Sin, or character defects, the seventh step of AA is an imposter and would not be a part of any journey ending in sobriety for the alcoholic. If we can fix ourselves Jesus wasted His time very painfully and the Bible makes no sense.

A "low view of Sin" and "cheap grace" are joy-stealing thieves. They disable our thought-life's ability to properly interpret suffering. A "low view of Sin" and "cheap grace" keep us working for a righteousness that pleases God instead of depending on God for our righteousness. God is pleased when we depend on Him for our righteousness. A deeper understanding of humility reveals how the two robbers of "a low view of Sin" and "cheap grace" make off with our freedom.

Chapter 10

Humble Freedom- There is No Other Kind

A thought-life immersed in the freedom of humility can accept suffering without being defined by it. Some good descriptions of humility are essential to exploring the complexities of suffering:
- Humility is not thinking less of yourself but thinking of yourself less.
- Humility is when "wants" meet "needs."
- Humility is simply seeing the truth.
- Humility is the absence of pride. If you think you're humble you're not.
- Humility is being grateful for the pain that brings surrender.

These are all very functional and accurate observations regarding humility but the last definition is the expression of humility that stands above all others. The deepest humility is being grateful for the pain. This definition of humility is where the deepest rubber meets the deepest road.

For the believer, Jesus' atonement for our sins means the suffering of life is not punishment from God for sins committed. Faith in Jesus' atonement allows the believer to accept life's sufferings as God's way of illuminating the path to a more steadfast joy. Suffering is sometimes consequence and other times not, but as a believer I must have faith all my suffering has purpose. There is so much comfort and peace in that confidence.

I would never intentionally inflict pain upon my child unnecessarily and I must believe God is as least as good a parent as I am. Jesus made this point.[39] Jesus called God "father." He taught us to pray, "Our Father." I know my heavenly Father limits my suffering as much as possible intellectually but in the middle of the suffering my arrogance makes me feel as though I'm being outright punished, not taught, or discipled, or matured. (When I feel this way it's a clue as to why I might be suffering.) The path to greater freedom always passes through the sanctification of painful self-examination brought on by life happening. There are just no shortcuts. Yes, true humility is being grateful for the pain. Are you grateful for the pain? I can only wish.

The human thought-life is a vacuum. The measure of our faith can be expressed by the ratio of pride to humility occupying this vacuum as our thought-life interprets our circumstances. Faith God is always acting in our best interest powers acceptance. Humility begets acceptance.

Freedom is found in our thought-life, not in our circumstances. Our thought-life, or our spiritual condition, is the commentary we make to ourselves regarding our circumstances. A thought-life drenched in

---

[39] Matthew 6:28

humility marks a joyous life. It shields us healthfully from the destructive messages sent by a "works righteousness world." A thought-life that sends us the right messages is the ultimate coping mechanism. It's the Godly coping mechanism that can be the source of true freedom. It is the only coping mechanism without a downside.

A joy-stealing conversation in our brains springs from one poisoned well- pride (aka self-centered fear). When humility yields to pride, when works righteousness brings on cheap grace, we find ourselves back under the law. The unavoidable process of sanctification is going back under the law and coming back out again. For the believer it's not "if" going back under the law happens. It's "when" it happens. Righteousness by faith frees us. Our quid pro quo brains, because they are broken, move us back under the law and into the grasp of the enslaving arrogance of works righteousness. The suffering of self sufficiency inspires us back into grace when we decide we've had enough. The process of sanctification is how God teaches us to enjoy the freedom of relying on Him not ourselves. Over the years, through sanctification, we are constantly becoming aware of our different righteousness schemes. Through sanctification our hidden addictions, our faulty righteousness schemes, boil to the surface.

Under law our thought-life sends wrong messages. These wrong messages share an insidious foundation. Under law our self esteem needs propping up constantly.

The unhappy art of comparison is always handy for the purposes of faulty self-esteem enhancement. Unable to produce humility in our *quid pro quo* brains, we make our level of self-esteem feel accentuated by comparing ourselves to others. "Comparing" is a derivative of the law-keeping and reputation-building righteousness schemes. It happens consciously and unconsciously to every human.

Determining who we should be and how we should feel based on comparisons is a dastardly, vicious and stealthy self-defeater. Comparing our works righteousness to others' work righteousness is a joy thief. It brings us pride in the form of arrogance and self-pity. Both feel soothing in the moment.

Self pity is nothing more than the arrogance of thinking we deserve better. Self-pity is often confused with humility. There is zero humility in self-pity. Those mired in self-pity often confuse humility with humiliation. They are unable to associate self-pity and low self-esteem with pride. Self-pity is a product of feeling unforgiven while operating under the law. Self-pity springs from a perception of injustice. Those aware of their Sin and their righteousness schemes don't feel injustice. The forgiven don't pity themselves.

Even the most faithful believers find themselves on the freeway of life dealing with idiots driving slower and maniacs zooming by faster. When we are in the default mode of "works righteousness" the comparisons we make force the person God made us to be into hiding. We project our perceptions onto our fellows. They must be comparing too, right? Self-esteem by comparison forces us into the prison of posing. We pose to solicit the affirming feedback our needy self-esteem demands.

The casualty on the "battlefield of comparing" is our "real self," the person God knitted together in the womb, the person God made us to be. "Works righteousness," whether "working" to please God or "working" to suck approval from others, or both, buries the person we really are and hobbles our God-given talents and gifts. To accomplish our goals using "works righteousness" requires us to wear finely-crafted masks. Most of the time our masks become so finely crafted we can't even tell we're wearing them.

Here are a few heart evaluation tools to help determine if you are under the law and wearing a finely crafted mask:

- In the last year how often did you utter the words, "I am/was wrong" without caveat, excuse or explanation?
- In the last year how often did you make a mistake and admit it before it was known to others?
- How often and how well do you defend yourself?
- How practiced is your talent for blame-shifting?
- How often do you sacrifice for someone without the news leaking?
- How often do you let someone take some of your credit?

- How often do you decide not to point out someone else's error (to them or someone else)?
- How much do you relish someone else's error?
- How much do you enjoy being right?
- How often do you demand to be judged on your intentions when confronted with your mistakes?
- How much do you enjoy a good ole' fashion demand for justice in regards to others?
- How often do you tell the story to make yourself look good, or at least better?
- How often to you justify and rationalize your bad decisions?
- How often do you avoid conflict to keep the peace?
- How often do you feel like a victim?
- How often do you feel God is disappointed with you?
- How often do you feel God is giving you less than you deserve?
- How deeply do you feel your record of behavior makes you a "good person"?
- How is your prayer life these days?
- How well do you wear the world as a loose garment?
- How often do you laugh at yourself?
- What is the count in your inventory of secrets today?
- Are you really grateful for the pain as God peals your fingers from your death grip on the things that make you miserable?

    Honesty is a tough gig.

Our brains, our built-in forgetters, get convinced taking off the mask is not vital to our happiness. Our works righteousness default mode gets locked in. A low view of Sin fools us into thinking we can "obey" enough to get by. We get proven wrong. When the pain we should be grateful for gets unbearable those being sanctified fall back into humble reliance on God's grace. Freedom is found again. We find freedom never moved, we did. More humility happens. Nothing breeds humility like realizing how reliable our built-in forgetters are.

Understanding God's grace, and incorporating the concept into our thought-life, just seems too simple a solution. Biblical principles, particularly those expressed through the 12 Steps of AA, demonstrate the human complexities preventing us from enjoying the full potential of God's grace are issues of humility. There is no better place to witness the contrast of life lived in humble freedom and life lived under the law than in Alcoholics Anonymous.

Chapter 11

Life Under The Law

The program of Alcoholics Anonymous has a spiritual recipe for a willing person to experience a change in behavior using the vehicle of faith. The "recipe" is a mixture of accepting certain suppositions and taking confirming steps. Undeniably the Church struggles to articulate a "therapy" to change destructive behavior worthy of universal implementation. The Church strives mightily to address the besetting sinful practices plaguing today's congregations, (pornography to mention a baffler), but really has no practical, dependable protocol acknowledged to be Biblical.

There are certain fundamentals of Biblical "behavior change" evident in the AA experience generally ignored by the Church. A look at the role Steps 6 and 7 play in the AA recovery process will be immensely helpful.

The most effectual prayer in my experience is the plea "God help me!" After other solutions are tried, the paradoxical power of surrendering to God is there. God's demand for surrender seems to put the "God solution" at the end of our solutions list when it comes to the mystery of finding a way to forsake unwanted, destructive behavior. "They could quit if they really wanted to" is a false statement according to the Bible (Romans 7). That power comes through surrender makes no sense to the wisdom of men. Surrendering to win is the purest spiritual paradox.

Conversely, the most ineffectual prayers in my experience ring like this: "God help me to .....," fill in the blank. "God, help me to stop watching pornography." "God, help me to get my eating disorder under control." "God help me to stop drinking." Prayers of this flavor produce rare enduring results in my experience. These are "counterpunch" prayers. There is an element of surrender missing. They are a-low-view-of-Sin prayers. They are Armenian prayers. They are prayers of the legalist.

I've never witnessed an answer to these prayers that brought about the desired result, at least not the result envisioned by the person making the prayer. Fundamentally, should such prayers bring about the desired result, God would have to share His glory with the benefactor. It goes back to the humility thing. When prayerful petitions leave room for ambiguity regarding how much of the good result (behavior change) is due to the benefactor's self-efforts (will power/works righteousness) and how much is due to God's grace, a sovereign God appears to remain largely unmoved.

Most newcomers to AA are agnostic or claim to have always had some "cultural belief" in God. Those raised in the Church more often than not bring a "Scarlet O'Hara faith" into the rooms of AA. When asked by Rhett about her belief in hell Scarlet replies in the affirmative explaining, "I was raised on it."[40] Scarlet epitomizes the feckless faith of cultural Christianity. The AA program anticipates these belief systems and deals with them successfully.

Churches and their keepers of doctrine have to admit AA has been dealing effectively with the Church's failures in treating substance abuse for some 85 years now. Shockingly, incomprehensibly, Christian "intellectuals" refuse to engage and blatantly refuse to take their head from the sand to consider what AA demonstrates. It's very sad. An antidotal survey shows these scholars think AA is self-help, group therapy, or something along those lines.

Unquestionably, it takes a lot of faith to pray for God to act alone in taking away the desire to sin, besetting sin certainly notwithstanding. It takes a lot of faith to understand, then act on, the notion that being under the law arouses the sinful desires of addiction.[41] Admittedly, it takes faith to leave out the "help me to" in prayers for behavior change. In my experience, however, such reliance on God seems to move Him. He gets the glory.

The Gospel just couldn't be that good though could it? God only helps those who help themselves, right? Funny, I can't find any such passages of Scripture in my Bible. To ignore the Biblical paradox that power

---

[40] Reference is to characters in Margaret Michell's novel *Gone With The Wind* (Macmillan Co. 1936)

[41] Romans 7:5

comes through weakness is a bad mistake. To sell God short is an even worse mistake. To those outside AA, believe what you will, but AA does not sell God short. Since we have seen that the Steps of AA use the "righteousness by faith" elements of the Gospel how they are used should be instructive.

The effect of alcohol on the alcoholic is the settling of guilt and shame into a calming righteousness. AA's approach to addressing the ill-gotten righteousness provided by the effects of alcohol to the alcoholic is transferable to addressing other addictions to ill-gotten righteousness, but in an unexpected way. Many think applying the principles of AA to other besetting sins requires manipulation of the 12 Steps. Just substituting whatever the besetting sin might be for alcohol into the wording of AA's first step misses what AA proves true.

AA's first three steps are often summarized: "I can't, He can, I think I'll let Him."[42] This summarization is a glimmering confirmation that the disease concept brings the willing alcoholic out from under the law. Granted the liberation is only regarding alcoholism but that's AA's concern. AA demonstrates being out from under the law is the top-shelf spiritual gear needed to address self-destructive behavior. Addiction is characterized by doing things we don't want to do over and over. Remember, in Romans 7 Paul tells us these kind

---

[42] *Alcoholics Anonymous*, p 60

of sinful desires are aroused by the law. AA's successful use of the disease concepts confirms what Paul wrote in Romans 7.

The Church, and some in AA, can't forsake adding the admonition, "try harder" to any behavior-change recipe. They fail to understand the admonition is dreadfully harmful. Adding "just try harder" kills any chance for success in achieving freedom from addiction. "Just try harder" is a righteousness scheme any way you cut it.

The AA experience offers a unique opportunity to observe the contrast between the self-help solution and the God solution. After being exposed to the truth that faith in Christ's atonement could bring me out from under the law completely, I realized my AA program had evolved into a "just try harder" theology. The mission of trusting God was now a mission to please God with my efforts. Everyone who has experienced the life changing grace of God comes upon the same challenge in developing spiritual maturity- staying out from under the law and its *quid pro quo*. Dealing with life after the pink cloud of being newly sober, without the disease concept having me out from under the law in all areas of life, my thought-life sunk back into the "works righteousness" mode.

The road to spiritual maturity inevitably forks. One path leads to a striving to please God. The other path leads to a striving to trust God. After four years in the pink cloud of AA sobriety, my thinking evolved into correlating my level of happiness and freedom with my ability to "work" the "maintenance" steps of AA; Steps 10, 11, and 12. This attitude developed over time. There was no day of decision like putting down the substance. Getting sucked back under the law was kind of like boiling a frog by putting it in a pot of cool water and placing it on a burner. Enjoying the cool water the frog becomes complacent. As the water slowly heats to the boiling point the frog is overcome before the threat of death motivates an escape. Like the frog, I went down without a fight. Modern day AA methodology did not warned me to be on the lookout for the law.

    The process of taking back control, reversing the third step and ignoring the seventh step in a manner of speaking, is the sure destination of one being sanctified in AA. Viewing the last three steps to be maintenance steps is a primrose path. Such a belief is common in the rooms of AA and reading the last three steps reveals why so many in AA believe these steps have a "maintenance" nature. Allowing the development of such an attitude to go unchecked is an easy mistake. Being powerless, growing character defects, confessing, asking God to remove shortcomings and making amends are the principles referenced in Step 12. My thought-life started telling me to try harder to be "honest" and try harder to be "willing." The "ends" of early sobriety became the "means" of maintenance steps. I was back under the law for sure.

    After several years in the AA program, I came to the conclusion I worked the last three steps quite well, all things considered, most of the time, thank you very much. Any humility resulting from my beginnings in AA had mostly slipped away. Now I know why.

    My sobriety went from being a gift to something I had earned and then into something I had to continually earn. Gratitude, and the humility it produces, diminished as I tried to be "honest" and "willing." Unconscientiously, I began to wear a more tightly fitting mask to AA meetings and in my relationships with others outside AA.

    Unwanted life circumstances and emotional tumult were attributed to "inadequate step working." There is no pink cloud in that sky. It's sublime slavery in sobriety. Forgetting the first seven steps make Step 12's "practice these principles in all our affairs" jail. The "inventory" word in Steps 4 and 10 can get nullified when "these principles" are not understood to be that of growing defects of character past sinful acts. When an examination of heart-level motives gets left out there is trouble on the horizon. A moral inventory (Step 4) is about sinful acts. A personal inventory (Step 10) is about heart-level motives. Step 12 can put you back under the law in a hurry if you're not careful. The Step 11 word "power" can get misconstrued. That's a land mine too.

Step 11 baffled me for a long time. "Praying only for the knowledge of God's will and the power to carry it out" was right there on the end of the Step. Yet every AA meeting I have ever attended has been closed by the Lord's Prayer. As we stood to hold hands and say the Lord's Prayer I thought, "Wait! I thought we were to pray only for the knowledge of God's will and the power to carry it out!" The Lord's Prayer at the end of the meeting was obviously in conflict with Step 11. I knew the Big Book is full of different prayers. What was going on here?

I chalked up the contradictions to well-intentioned traditions and considered the obvious conflicts not important. After I was exposed to Reformed theology it dawned on me. The "power" in Step 11 is really humility. I completely understand why the step doesn't read the "powerlessness" to carry out God's will but, in effect, that's what AA theology teaches. Considered in this light, the meeting-ending Lord's Prayer and the many prayers contained in the Big Book are a practice of acknowledging powerlessness. They fit majestically in Step 11. Forgetting the paradox that power comes from powerlessness will lead to misconstruing Step 11. Confusion about power will also lead to big problems in Step 12.

There's no freedom pass being sober living life with misconstrued Steps 11 & 12. The slippery slope of self-reliance greased by hidden addictions is mighty slick. Righteously working the steps and regularly attending meetings hoping God would reward me with less suffering (as oppose to relying on God for an unshakable joy to benefit from suffering), starts to take on a deceptively logical rationale. Having a thought-life sending messages of "just try harder" is no fun. There's no freedom in it.

The trap of "self-reliance" is a very wide pit. The world incessantly hammers us with reinforcements of the *quid pro quo* notion and maturing members of AA are particularly susceptible. The disease concept doesn't apply past alcohol. That's not a commentary on the vibrance of AA. Going back under the law is just easier to discern in AA because when sobriety gets taken for granted the recovered alcoholic, absent the Gospel, is de facto back under the law.

Incredibly, and inexplicably, experiencing God's power and glory is a fleeting lesson-learned in the human mind. The compulsion to earn our own righteousness to fill the God-shaped hole, the human's fatal flaw, is resilient beyond comprehension. A short memory is the enfeeblement of every person hoping to grow spiritually.

The angst of being under the law feels natural. According to the world the "accomplished," the "talented," are capable of fulfilling their deepest desires and eliminate the God-shaped hole in their beings using ingenuity and sweat. You get what you earn. What goes around comes around. If you want righteousness, act righteously. The world constantly sends these messages.

Our short memories, our built-in forgetters, have lots of help. Madison Avenue understands that breeze blowing through our God-shaped emptiness perfectly. Understanding it is a science. Advertisers expertly exalt the "righteousness" of their wares. They peddle the good things in life that we deserve or can't live without. They promise to make us feel better about ourselves. Their unspoken guarantee is a filled God-shaped void.

Marketers use "reputation righteousness," "sex righteousness," "wealth righteousness," "house righteousness," "car righteousness," "toothpaste righteousness," "pet righteousness," "deodorant righteousness," "you-name-it righteousness," to convince us how deserving we are, or how their product will make us deserving, or meet our human vacuum's demand for earned righteousness. Successful ad campaigns depend on striking the right cord in the sin-soaked human default mode of the *quid pro quo* and the need for the righteousness it produces.

"You can have our super duper mouse trap for the low, low price of $9.95. But wait! For a limited time we'll add a second super duper mouse trap at no cost in this very special offer!" We know we're being lied to about the price of a super duper mouse trap. We know it's not a special offer but it doesn't matter. Advertisers understand our sub conscience *quid pro quo* loves that free second mouse trap and that love even trumps the hesitancy of buying something from a liar.

Life Under The Law

The list of our "righteousness vulnerabilities" and the opportunities to indulge them is endless. We learn about this list and such opportunities very early in life. Starting around age three my youngest daughter, "the informer," would appear to "drop a dime" on her older siblings at the slightest provocation. Being less skilled at everything, this toddler could earn herself some sweet righteousness playing tattletale. To be found "most obedient" was the righteousness prize. The temporary ire of the older siblings she worshiped was worth it, just a cost of doing "righteousness" business.

In the smoking area at work John finds a half-eaten apple left on a picnic table. John never finished high school having spent most of his teenage years in prison. Being somewhat of a "neat freak," he reacts to the half-eaten apple by demanding only coworkers found to be tidy enough be given permission to eat in the smoking area. Believing a neatness test is one he can pass that others might fail he ceases on the opportunity for some "apple righteousness." John is not really concerned with getting the apple, or future apples, in the trash as much as he is making everyone aware that he would never be caught in such a malfeasance. By creating the biggest possible stir, John is able to temporarily fill his God-shaped hole by flaunting his "apple righteousness." As is the case with even the most sophisticated righteousness schemes, the fulfillment John derived from his "apple righteousness" was a costly vapor. He managed to insult all his coworkers in one fell swoop. Just the cost of doing "righteousness" business.

Reporting the news has moved from a journalistic endeavor to exercises in bloviating to attract righteousness seekers with a certain political view. Espousing the right interpretation of political events is a neat way to infer those in disagreement to be of lesser discernment. The conservatives watching Fox News or the liberals watching CNN sit soaking up the righteousness that comes from affirmation of their point of view. Unbiased news is by the wayside. Advertisers have learned to have the television news cast tells us what we pay it to tell us. It's a new way to monetize the human need for righteousness. That objective journalism has become extinct is just a cost of doing "righteousness" business.

The human susceptibility to the righteousness con is as reliable as one's relationship to Adam. We fall for it over and over again. My three year old was unassailable for helping enforce the house rules and quick to claim that motive. In John's mind his motive was to keep the smoking area clean for the enjoyment of all. Bewildered by the opposition's lack of reason, the news-consuming public is motivated to save the world by vanquishing the opposition's idiocy. Road rage is a "go to" righteousness scheme for many. Righteousness in our own eyes feels so good. It's addictiveness can't be matched or overstated.

Operating with the belief we have the power to follow God's law then failing to do so leaves a righteousness void we must fill with something. Like the wind across the plain, episodes of temporary works righteousness victories blow across our self-perceptions never sticking. The hunt for the next sibling infraction, the next apple, the next outrage by the political opposition, never ends. The need for righteousness is a thirst never quenched under the law. Only faith that we are no longer under the law deals with our addiction to earned righteousness. **This is what Paul means when he talks about the law arousing sinful desires. Under the law there is no righteousness outside our personal renditions of misbehaving siblings, half-eaten apples and political idiots.**

In the unavoidable cycle of sanctification, at a point where we've taken back control, we deal with latent misery or stand at attention to the sharp pain of some crisis. The pain moves us. We reach for the earned righteousness that brings us comfort. It's how we temporarily fix ourselves.

The short relief period of having the comfort of some earned righteousness blocks out our feelings of inadequacy just long enough to put surrender a little farther out of reach. Acquiescing to filling our God-shaped holes with temporary earned righteousness is addiction. Addiction tells us temporary relief is better than nothing. It decays our faith and robs us of our freedom. Its progression is the lesson about-to-boil frogs teach.

All humans are controlled by this "instinct" to fill our God-shaped holes with what works.... for us. Under the law unrecognized righteousness schemes control the conversation in our thought-life. We hustle to quench our wants as though others will not replace them immediately. The quest to fill the God-shaped hole in our psyche is an ever-present crisis only temporarily appeased by things "outside us." Under law, our need to earn righteousness drives us to audition most anything for the role of being our God substitute. Stuck in the desert with a bunch of gold we'll mold it into a calf then kneel down and worship it. We will worship it because we created it. Our golden calves are evidence of our goodness, of our righteousness earned.

Chapter 12

Taking Right Steps In The Wrong Direction

  I am certain my AA experience is fairly typical. With the passage of time and without the Gospel, the program of AA brought me a disguised arrogance. AA has its own brand of Pharisee. After several years recovered alcoholics without the Gospel and with a low view of Sin develop a shorter and shorter list of character defects and the smaller and smaller need for God that comes with that shrinking list. It's the quintessential return to being under the law. In regards to legalism, AA works in a particular, predictable way.

  The freedom found in early sobriety dissipates with time. Loss of gratitude is a natural progression as the pink cloud of a new spiritual awakening morphs into a familiar sobriety that starts being taken for granted. An alcoholic's abstinence does not thwart the passage of time nor life's painful challenges. Life becomes a harder and harder reality as gratitude wanes. Aged sobriety born in today's rooms of AA breed a return to the methods that produced the original joy of early sobriety's spiritual awakening- the 12 Steps. It's a sneaky righteousness scheme that doesn't work.

  Reworking the steps, going to more meetings, finding a different home group, becoming the meeting coffee maker again, getting involved in service work, may all be "good" things but none are the solution suggested in the first 164 pages of the Big Book. AA meetings are not even mentioned in the first 164 pages of the Big Book. A suggestion to rework the steps is nowhere to be found either.

Many in AA prescribe a second fourth and fifth step when the inevitable spiritual malaise of sanctification hits. It's a logical but ineffective solution not prescribed by the AA program. When the 12 Steps turn into works righteousness they become a human solution. Deploying the old tools to gin a new spiritual awakening or create a new pink cloud is like trying to put smoke in your pocket. Being under the law is sneaky problem, especially when no one is on guard against it.

If the success of AA recovery hinged on a "work righteousness" theology and "works righteousness" could break the funk, working the steps again would get the job done. The original measures used to bring about an AA spiritual awakening and the subsequent pink cloud would be sound, sobriety freshening tools. Steps 10, 11 and 12 are the Big Book's answer. The click in that starter is that without the righteousness by faith aspects of Steps 6 and 7 works righteousness overwhelms the "practice these principles in all our affairs" commemoration in Step 12. Steps 6 and 7 blow up the law. They can't be forgotten.

Steps 6 and 7 void any works righteousness interpretation of Steps 10, 11 and 12 when understood. While all the other Steps have pages of explanation, Steps 6 and 7 garner only one paragraph each in the Big Book.

This is AA genus. The human default to works righteousness was blunted by subtraction. Seems the Big Book anticipates recovering alcoholics will wrongly come around to "reworking" Steps 4 and 5 to freshen their sobriety. The examination of Steps 6 and 7 also reveals why Steps 10, 11 and 12 are found lacking as maintenance steps; growth steps yes, maintenance steps, no. As maintenance steps 10, 11 and 12 are a Pharisee's dream come true.

  Step 6 is "were entirely ready to have God remove all these defects of character." The "step" is one of recognition. The first word "were" is past tense. To "work this step" requires time travel. The Big Book says Step 6 is about willingness, willingness that comes from growing our character defects in Steps 4 and 5.[43] Step 6 is not about manufacturing willingness!!!! Step 6 is about recognizing God has used the first five steps to produce willingness!

  Step 6 and 7 are analogous to a child unable to swim, who has never jumped into a swimming pool. Ready to take on the challenge, the child stands on the edge of the pool in front of the outstretched arms of an encouraging parent. The encouraging parent makes repeated promises of immediate rescue while promoting the fun to be had. The child flexes his knees in simulated launch. With fear and apprehension the child looks around

---

[43] Ibid, p. 76

to see scores of children jumping in the pool with no fear and experiencing joyful exhilaration. The child desperately wants the freedom to join in the fun but the "testimony" of the other children only serves to mitigate the fear, not wipe it away.

Step 6 is the willingness to don the swimsuit and stand next to the pool's edge. The child would have no conception of a swimming pool had the circumstances of life not worked to make the revelation. The child didn't build the swimming pool.

Bending his knees, shuffling his feet on the pool's hard concrete edging, constantly looking down then up, he's willing but still dry. The child looks yearningly at the pool's steps which permit a slow emersion into the pool. Oh, the wonderful steps of the pool's corners where the foot feels the bottom and the pool's edge is never out of reach. But that's not the mission. Willingness has brought the child to the pool's edge for the purpose of jumping.

The child's only solution is the reckless abandonment of the dreaded jump. Step 6's "entirely" is coming to terms with the "all or nothing" nature of the "God proposition." As the Big Book says, *"half measures availed us nothing. We stood at the turning point. We asked His protection with complete abandon."*[44]

Step 7 is throwing self-sufficiency to the wind and stepping off into the pool despite not being able to swim. While works righteousness theologies would have us

---

[44] *Alcoholics Anonymous*, p. 59

flailing away to keep our head above water, "working" to find God's spot in the pool for support, the Bible and AA teach God will be there to catch us. Righteousness through faith promises a life of learning to swim with the undergirding hand of Almighty God always keeping us afloat. The picture is one of "letting go and letting God," free from being under the law. God isn't going to leave us to fin for ourselves no matter what if we can make the faithful, reckless jump. The willingness accumulated by the first six steps compels us to jump. There is no option.

"Willingness" for the AA newcomer isn't so hard. Giving up the misery of the recent maelstrom is no big deal really. No elaboration by the Big Book is necessary for the newcomer. For the AA veteran, Step 6 is a whole other can of worms. Being willing to move past a spiritual place in sobriety requires a different kind of desperation. The Big Book's brevity on Steps 6 and 7 turns into an honesty issue for the AA veteran. When Steps 10, 11, and 12 are growth steps the issues become centered around motives, not acts.

The one paragraph devoted to Step 7 in the Big Book is a prayer: "*My Creator, I am now willing that you should have all of me, good and bad. I pray that you now remove from me every single defect of character which stands in the way of my usefulness to you and my fellows. Grant me the strength, as I go out from here, to do your*

Why Alcoholics Anonymous Works

bidding. Amen."[45] God hears this kind of prayer for granting such a petition brings Him glory. There is not a trace of self-fixing in these words. This prayer is not a counterpunch.

Cleverly, Steps 6 and 7 bar any method of addressing spiritual drudgery using the "works righteousness" of any self-effort model. The Big Book's few words about Steps 6 and 7 avoid any confusion on this most important point. God removes character defects of the powerless, humble believer that has character defects. When mature members of AA do tenth steps and come up empty handed spiritual malaise has set in. Limiting Step 10's personal inventory to a reflection on behavior cleans up the process pretty good. Actually, a low view of Sin castrates Step 10.

To further the swimming pool analogy, Steps 6 and 7 don't elaborate on the nature of the encouraging parent but they cleverly eliminate the legalist. Step 7's reliance on God to remove shortcomings limits the parent in the pool to a "righteousness by faith" rescuer. Notice how logic excludes all but a Biblically Reformed defined parent? Humility, that thing we cannot produce, inspires God to remove "shortcomings." Steps 10, 11, and 12, fueled by efforts to be "willing" and "honest," or whatever, is works righteousness that violates the principle of Step 7. Step 7's reliance on God to remove

---

[45] Ibid., p. 76

shortcomings puts the kabash on using the last three steps as legalistic maintenance steps.

Steps 6 and 7, as does the whole Big Book, only describes God, the pool's encouraging parent, in somewhat generic terms. The AA methodology however is anything but generic. The righteousness by faith foundation of AA eliminates all but one answer to the quandary of who the parent waiting in the pool is. All the Steps, but Steps 6 and 7 in particular, require a God of grace. For the intellectually honest, the quandary is not a Buddha-answered quandary, or a Mohammad-answered quandary, or an Armenian-answered quandary, or an any-other-answered quandary. Step 7's humble request for God to remove one's shortcomings shucks the options of who is standing in the pool right down to the cob.

To get the real freedom God has to offer, to get the ginormous nugget of life, we must walk the plank. Poked and prodded by the pain of our life's wounds or the dullness of an unfulfilled spiritual life or plagued by a condemning conversation going on in our *quid pro quo* brains, having tried every other alternative which might offer relief, if we can stumble off the plank our landing will be into the sweetness of life. A radical surrender in sobriety brings a refreshed spirit. Being out from under the law again super-freshens worn sobriety into something very, very special. God's forgiveness is the force multiplier on humility and gratitude.

Jesus knows you can't swim. The Big Book knows you can't swim. The Big Book's receipt for spiritual growth, a refreshed sobriety, is found on page 87 in the discussion of Step 11, *"If we belong to a religious denomination which requires a definite morning devotion, we attend to that also. If not members of religious bodies, we sometimes select and memorize a few set prayers which emphasize the principles we have been discussing. There are many helpful books also. Suggestions about these may be obtained from one's priest, minister, or rabbi.* ***Be quick to see where religious people are right. Make use of what they offer.****"* (emphasis added).

I don't recall ever being in an AA meeting with this passage of the Big Book as the topic. It seems AA theology has evolved into "make use of what they offer" if you feel like it, or if you feel like you need it. "Make use of what they offer" is not a suggestion in the Big Book. A monolithic reliance on the Big Book is not the AA program of recovery. The miracle of sobriety is but a special seed. Watered by the Gospel it grows into a most distinguishing forest. Back under the law unwatered sobriety withers. It may still be sobriety but it withers.

Chapter 13

AA Alone

The fellowship of Alcoholics Anonymous, like the church, like any organization really, offers the opportunity of "organizational righteousness." Alcoholics Anonymous is not immune to the flaws that come with being populated by humans. The AA fellowship itself can be used as a temporary God substitute just as churchgoers use the church in the same wrong way.

Experience, the test of time if you will, has proven that AA, in and of itself, can become an imposter substituting for alcohol to the exclusion of the Creator. This is not a knock on AA in any way. The same sexy imposter appears in every single place that affords people the opportunity to "play spiritual" in lieu of practicing humble service. Worship of the church happens all the time. Being under the law brews the temporary relief of works righteousness even at God places. Legalism seeps into where ever folks find themselves.

Sobriety achieved through AA however brings a unique perspective to the works righteousness issue as experienced in such "spiritual" organizations. Because it is taken on science and not so much faith, the disease concept so completely takes the recovering alcoholic out from under the "sobriety law," any subsequent "sobriety legalism" sticks out like a sore thumb.

Just months into the journey of taking the 12 Steps, the recovering alcoholic feels hope from just being sober. Having the desire to drink in the rearview, humble gratitude abounds. The experience would logically put the alcoholic ahead on the spiritual maturity meter compared to someone investigating Christianity at the behest of a lesser desperation. God-dependence just works that way; bigger sin, bigger gift, bigger God.

Those who are capable, maybe even predisposed, may be able to think their way into right acting in the beginning of their spiritual journey. They are able to take the Church's remedy of swallowing some theology and make an inspired start. The alcoholic recovered in AA has acted his way into right thinking. He has taken the "being out from under the law" freedom of the disease concept and run with it. The two groups are in different places spiritually even if time seeking God is relatively equal.

Having lost all hope, having hope restored is a powerful, powerful development. The recovered alcoholic is naturally endowed with a superior gratitude. While certainly all suffering is relative, the serving of gratitude before the newly sobered alcoholic is a Thanksgiving feast. The rescue from alcoholism is of unique magnitude on the list of possible sanctifying life events.

There seems to be a trade off though. When righteousness through faith produces humility without the Gospel's doctrine of imputed righteousness there is a cap on spiritual growth that's not readily apparent. The disease concept is a single "get-out-of-jail-free card" only good on the turn of alcoholism.

I was not wrong to suspect the commitment of my friends at this Bible-believing church. God had not done for them what he had done for me. Their life did not depend on their spiritual condition so tangibly as did mine. Nevertheless, I was in a spiritual doldrum without a way forward. They had a way forward. To move into the realm of wider gratitude required the Gospel's doctrine of no longer being under the law spreading to all areas of my life. For me the gratitude of AA was like the power of an atomic explosion. The gratitude of the Gospel feels like the power of a vast ocean's permanence and reach.

The disease concept's nuclear explosion did not take me out from under the law past alcohol. Alcohol was no longer a problem (or solution) for me. I had the blessing of sobriety- a new life with new, unfamiliar problems. I needed the permanence and reach of a Mighty Ocean.

At first I thought the Gospel would finish baking my AA bread. My spirituality was dough with just the right amount of yeast to my thinking. I knew I was bread. I thought I had yeast. I may have even been heated up a little. At my introduction to the Gospel my vision was to have the Gospel just finish cooking me, just bake me at 350 Gospel degrees for an hour and my AA bread would rise to fill my God-shaped hole. Turns out, I was dough, no yeast. Personally, my spiritual condition was never going to rise to fill the God-shaped hole strictly on the AA doctrine of today. I was flat bread without liberation from being under the law in all areas of my life.

No disrespect to AA intended. Without Alcoholics Anonymous I would have never found myself in sober attendance at a Bible study. I promise you that. AA did for me everything the Big Book promised, and then some. What I required was the principles of AA, not being under the law, to be spread to all parts of my life. I needed to practice the right principles in all my affairs.

Charting a person's ability to live using a healthy thought-life as a primary coping mechanism looks like a stock market chart. Increasing without decreasing doesn't happen. Our broken thinkers see to it. Our short memories require the process of sanctification and its growing pains to scale life's spiritual mountains. It seems we have to go through the valleys of being under the law to appreciate being pulled out again.

Getting pulled out from under the law again is hard to happen in AA because being under the law isn't perceived as the problem. Architecturally, if Steps 10, 11 and 12 don't reflect Steps 6 and 7, there is no way forward spiritually. When the principles of Steps 6 and 7 are not applied to Step 12's "practice these principles in all our affairs" thought-lives get infected with works righteousness. With an infected twelfth step there is no spiritual way forward. It is easy to spin our wheels in the mud of works righteousness. When recovered alcoholics don't understand righteousness by faith the traction for being pulled out from under the law in regards to nonalcoholic issues isn't there.

The pink cloud fading is a natural thing. It's a sure thing. Dusty sobriety will raise the question of how much the recovered alcoholic is willing to learn about this God to whom they have decided to entrust with their lives. Being "willing to go to any lengths" never ends.

The open architecture of AA is genus. The architecture of AA is "open" because the Big Book's success comes even though the text avoids opining on what happens to humans at death. Death is in every human's windshield so speculation on the matter is universal and unavoidable. There is not a more germane question for mortals. **What we think about death effects the messages our thought-life sends us before death happens. This is another spiritual law.**

The certainty of death demands an answer to the Jesus question. As C.S. Lewis points out: "If Christianity is not true it is of no importance. If Christianity is true nothing can be more important. What Christianity can't be is moderately important." There is no intellectually cogent argument to dispute Mr. Lewis' observation. Christianity is not true if Jesus was just a great teacher or great philosopher because Jesus taught about His role pertaining to the afterlife.

Many recovered in AA decline Biblical exploration deciding sobriety is enough. It seems there is a pass given in AA against the mandate on page 87 of the Big Book. I get it. One huge miracle can surely define a person's life. A recovered alcoholic's "no" answer to the Jesus question is understandable. Part of their life's gratitude is that their solution to drunkenness comes from outside the Church's Bible gobbledygook and legalism. I get that too. There was a significant period of my life in which the Church and the Bible left me unaffected. For many in AA the Church's legalism made things worse. Legalism wounds, and wounds deeply.

Many who decline Biblical exploration get drunk as carelessness chokes their spiritual fitness. The AA experience feels like being out from under the law for awhile. **The sobered in AA rightly fear theologies that seek to religiously enslave them in legalism once again.** They wisely refuse to wear religious shackles. The shackles of AA legalism at least demand sobriety. AA shackles don't wound the recovered alcoholic like other legalistic shackles.

As the pink cloud of excitement in the newly sober inevitably gets absorbed into the reality of life, a decision will be made. Page 87 of the Big Book will be ignored or it won't. When page 87 gets ignored "a higher power" and the program of AA get hard to distinguish. Love of AA and the works righteousness it allows provides the success of avoiding the first drink. The obedience of sobriety (as opposed to the gift of sobriety) and the righteousness it brings obscures motives and matters of the heart. It's spiritual gravity.

    Living under AA law makes sobriety an invisible shackle. In society being a Pharisee is a lot better than being a drunk- a whole lot better. No greater understatement has ever been made. Unlike constant drunkenness, the sober lifestyle is economically and medically sustainable. But life is not about being sober. There are many sober nonalcoholics living in misery. Life is about loving and being loved.

    Ignoring page 87 is a big decision. Ignoring it corrupts what the Big Book proffers. The pull of AA is decidedly in the singular direction of investigating the Jesus question. Righteousness by faith attracts righteousness by faith. On pages 130-131, the Big Book hones what is said on page 87:

    "Though the family has no religious connections, they may wish to make contact with or take membership in a religious body.

    Alcoholics who have derided religious people will be helped by such contacts. Being possessed of a spiritual experience, the alcoholic will find he has much in common with these people, though he may differ with them on many matters. If he does not argue about religion, he will make new friends and is sure to find new avenues of usefulness and pleasure. He and his family can be a bright spot in such congregations. He may bring new hope and new courage to many a priest, minister, or rabbi, who gives his all to minister to our troubled world. We intend for the fore-going as a helpful suggestion only. So far as we are concerned, there is nothing obligatory about it. As non-denominational people, we cannot make up others' minds for them. Each individual should consult his own conscience."

We alcoholics clean up surprisingly well. In this passage the Big Book plainly endorses those with long-term sobriety returning to the Church. There is just no requirement to do so. The key line is, *"Each individual should consult his own conscience."* Failing to consult your own conscience is not the AA program of recovery.

Sadly, returning to Church is not always a good thing for those in recovery. In a legalistic congregation the recovered alcoholic runs into inconsistencies of doctrine. These churches try to slip recovered alcoholics back under the law. No one needs help in slipping back under the law. No one needs a push down that hill. To avoid using shame and guilt to "encourage" obedience requires constant vigilance. Advocating the use of will power to bring about changes in the heart denies the paradox of humility. There is no paradox in religious dogma demanding more self-effort.

The "spiritual dimming" in AA begins as an illusion of "goodness." Leaving the Step 6 and Step 7 quandaries unanswered limits God to the box of sobriety. Sovereignty over other areas of life, many new areas of life, is an authority vacuum that will be filled.

Unburdened by the chaos of the alcoholic lifestyle, the life that was unmanageable at sobriety's beginning curves into a seemingly manageable set of problems. Figuring out the exact nature of God and experiencing God lacks urgency as good things start to happen to the "good." It's no character flaw. Again, it's the principle of spiritual gravity. Desperation eludes about-to-boil frogs. The cycle of sanctification is not avoidable, in or out of AA.

As recovered alcoholics become better parents, better employees, better members of the community, and of society in general, the humility of God's grace fades into the calendar. The recovered alcoholic, just as the Israelites, just as anyone who has had a sharp encounter with God, starts to have recollection difficulties. God begins to need help. It's only a matter of time before we arrive at the end of our short memory. The process of sanctification guarantees the arrival of works righteousness in every spiritual journey, at several points in every spiritual journey actually. Works righteousness never gets whipped entirely. That would require perfect faith.

Sanctification, in the Church and in AA, are ebbs and flows between depending on God and not depending on God, on trusting God and using self-effort to please Him. The curse of Adam sucks us back under the law and God's grace pulls us out again. Unlike justification, sanctification is not a "one and done" thing. It's a cycle. The grace of sanctification is one of developing longer memories and less painful motivators as we collect life experiences of God proving worthy of our faith.

Ebbs in sanctification are not always marked by outward disobedience. Outward disobedience is an easy slavery to spot compared to the invisible works righteousness slavery that grows in our thought-life. The works righteousness that marks an ebb in sanctification always starts in our thought-life. Works righteousness appears under deep cover. By the time condemning messages from our thought-life announce its arrival, works righteousness has established a foothold. Condemning messages hit our *quid pro quo* brains long before outward disobedience happens. Outward disobedience (loss of freedom) is fruit of the legal tree fertilized by our hidden schemes to acquire ill-gotten righteousness.

Obedience (sobriety in the alcoholic's case) springs from gratitude or pride. An ebb in sanctification is obedience motivated by gratitude devolving into obedience born of pride. It is out the pride window that freedom flies. The prideful obedience that looks so good on the outside feels like a duty kept on the inside. The world begins to feel heavy. Freedom fades.

The truth that never-before-detected motives get found in the valleys of life and not the mountain tops gets proved over and over. When our outsides look obedient the pressure to change gets left unchambered. Painful self-examination is just not possible on emotional mountain tops. It's just not. There are no short cuts to discovering our self-deceiving methods and motives. Our little schemes for procuring righteousness hide so well in our thought-life. They are masters of disguise.

When our outsides look obedient and blessings flow we can lose our freedom fast. Pride ceases our thinkers. Sanctification resets thinkers. Humility is being grateful for the pain that resets thinkers and restores freedom. In the humility window freedom flies.

"Reputation righteousness," "church righteousness," "doctrinal righteousness," "AA righteousness," are the most perplexing forms of enslavement for the person seeking God's freedom. The deep honesty required to identify such righteousness schemes is hard and most of the time requires forfeiture of long held beliefs. These phony righteousness procurement strategies are incredibly well-disguised addictions. The denial that comes with addiction is a mysterious and powerful thing.

Collectively, let's label "reputation righteousness," "church righteousness," and "AA righteousness" as "law-keeping righteousness" addiction. The ever-sly "law-keeping righteousness" is a type of righteousness Jesus warns against most virulently.[46] My "law-keeping righteousness" had me believing I was a "good" person before being introduced to Reformed theology. It also had

---

[46] Matthew 6 is just one citation out of many, many options.

me believing the Big Book was more profound than the Bible. It had me believing a compromising God was much more, vastly more, loving than a just God. These were long held beliefs I forfeited breaking out of a very dull valley in sobriety.

Law-keeping inspired by pride is a stealthy monster. It looks so good on us and hides motives of the heart so well. On the outside law-keeping righteousness is very, very hard to distinguish from righteousness by faith. On the outside, obedience reveals only so much about the heart. The once disobedient now enjoying the fruits of obedience have a way of becoming agnostic regarding heart issues. It's a comfort thing. It's an if-it-ain't-broke-don't-fix-it thing. It's an easier-softer-way thing.

The level of honesty required to shine light into the dark places of "law-keeping righteousness" is a spiritual discernment of the highest order. As God would have it, this level of honesty, this spiritual discernment, is reserved for those blessed with an ability to respond to life with a certain attitude. "Law-keeping righteousness" appears to be a victimless crime but it's not. The law-keeper is not free and a chained heart is a calloused, loveless ache that effects all relationships.

A very good example and illustration of a stealthy law-keeper addiction is the churchgoer sporting "Bible righteousness" as a preferred flavor of law-keeping righteousness. It's a very educational example. It's a glimpse into how law-keeping righteousness conceals itself so effectively.

This person shows up on Sunday, every Sunday, to worship service clasping an old, worn out Bible. Sunday church just wouldn't be the same without this Bible. The cover is all crinkled. What was once a shiny black cover could now pass for zebra skin. On the pages are marks and notes everywhere. The binding is so loose this Bible can't be opened in the slight breeze of an air conditioning vent. The "Old Rock" is in such bad shape family and friends have given the perfect gift- a new Bible to replace it. None see the light of day.

This person would be highly offended at the suggestion carrying such a Bible is motivated by law-keeping righteousness. The need to offer proof of piety and suck approval from fellow churchgoers could not be this sacred Bible's purpose. It's too worn, obviously. A righteous rebuke is due any blasphemous heretic who might make any such allegation disrespecting the Word of God. This person is incensed at any insinuation the unread notes in the margin aren't vital. Making a defense of carrying the worn Bible is easy and a warmness whelms up inside as it is given.

The crinkled-covered Bible feeds the ego and is a source of pride. The tattered ole Word helps create the reputation of a diligent student of Scripture and standing as a "good person." A "bad person" could not possibly be the owner of a Bible in this condition.

In fact, this person needs this crinkled covered Bible more than God. The dishonest blindness of law-keeping righteousness and worship of reputation has robbed this person's freedom. They don't believe the long-nurtured Bible holds an inappropriate place in their life or in their faith. They are cocksure it doesn't. Blindly they believe carrying such a Bible is an act of faith, not an act of works righteousness.

The Bible's display of piety provides righteousness to temporarily fill the God-shaped hole. This person can't wait for Sunday service. Walking into church carrying the Bible feels good even if no one notices its condition. Sadly, the crinkle-covered Bible acts to muffle the Spirit's call to journey into a "motives examination."

Be sure this Bible righteousness scheme doesn't live alone in the schemer's heart. Bible righteousness is just one of many sly righteousness schemes that come in this package. When resting on God's abilities is forfeited for resting on our own abilities the bondage is never confined to one compartment of life.

This person is completely unaware they choose the prison of work righteousness over real freedom. Real freedom stands out of sight in an unlit corner of the heart and goes undiscovered. This person is unable to love deeply or be loved deeply though they crave love badly. They are baffled as to why love is so illusive. Piety fits

AA Alone

their mask tightly. Their mask is getting the love not them and they feel it.

One day, walking through some valley, pain will bring this person to their knees and the scales will drop from their eyes as they come to the end of themselves. If they are lucky.

In AA, length of time maintaining continuous sobriety can be the proverbial crinkled-covered Bible. It pours nicely into the mold of a shinny golden calf. Long-term sobriety is a qualification for dispensing AA wisdom and the length of sobriety the measuring tape of success. Any awareness that God was more indispensable in early sobriety than after twenty years provides no insight. The seminal crisis of life seems to have passed. And for many it has.

AA meetings can provide a place-holder for God. They present the opportunity to have the law-keeping righteousness of long-term sobriety stoked and stroked. AA law-keeping righteousness is a special variety that has the proven ability to elongate prideful obedience in the form of long-term sobriety. As sobriety is put on the books day after day this earned righteousness becomes a bigger and bigger threat to the real spiritual growth produced only when gratitude grows. God becomes distant and dull but the appearance of success sustains as the streak of days without a drink gets put on the books.

Staying sober can get confused with trusting God. The ability to love gets harder if sobriety produces pride. Sobriety can be a well-fitted mask.

AA law-keeping righteousness, more often than not, sooner or later, makes extending the length of sobriety more important than expanding the relationship with God. When taking self identity from length of sobriety, the specter of breaking the streak of days without a drink keeps many an alcoholic dry. Everybody in the program knows how much sobriety everyone else has. AA has a first class pecking order and even those with minimal sobriety know it. As dependence on God trickles away the void can be filled by the righteousness of an unfulfilling AA perch.

Too much "store" in length of sobriety stagnates the pond of AA spiritual growth. "Sobriety righteousness" blinds. Page 87 of the Big Book is ignored on the easy calculation a richer God experience is inferred to be at the end of the more-sobriety rainbow. It's easy not to notice the Big Book never promises spiritual maturity will be the product of long-term sobriety.

The long-recovered alcoholic might concede desperation for God is less than in those days of early sobriety. They may even admit this lack of desperation makes what might be beneficial Biblical exploration feel unnecessary. On the relatively calm seas of sobriety, finding freedom by discovering buried motives, and developing the ability to love that comes with it, has no urgency. It does not appear such discoveries offer any great reward. Again, a low view of sin castrates Step 10.

Diminishing freedom experienced by getting sober can endure into the cobwebs of time. After the "Great Enlightenment of Sobriety," the AA old-timer, refusing to Biblically engage, nurturers the residual drops of gratitude dripping from the ever-drying AA foliage.

When life hits the fan, if prideful sobriety is present, it feels deep down as though God isn't keeping his end of the *quid pro quo* bargain. Suffering isn't beneficial. It feels like being cheated, however subconsciously. Victimhood is an untenable state for the God-dependent. The time to fish or cut bait will come. Life's pain will bring more "law" (trying harder) or more grace (letting go and letting God). **Under grace pain is the great distiller of humility. Under law pain distills a resolution to try harder still.**

These are the spiritual principles that show trying to grow spiritually with wrong ideas about Steps 10, 11 and 12, leaves one under the law with no spiritual way forward. When sobriety comes without answering the Jesus question it's easy to ignore the question. The question appears to have been sidestepped. Never having been exposed to the true nature and purpose of God's law can make the Jesus question appear to be not pertinent. Saying "no" to the Jesus question doesn't appear to rob freedom. Those old voices of prejudice tell the recovering alcoholic that freedom is robbed on the "yes" side of the Jesus question.

Understanding how we source law-keeping righteousness is the toughest spiritual discernment for both the churchgoer and the alcoholic recovered in AA. Unhappiness, discontentment and self-pity are sure signs we are improperly sourcing righteousness. For those in recovery exactly how righteousness is being sourced is a hard, hard question only answered in a properly done 10th step. The new varieties of false righteousness that come with sobriety are pink elephants of a different color.

What has been said about righteousness and righteousness schemes is easily confirmed to the AA old-timer. AA's spiritual crown jewel is proof AA is about righteousness by faith. The principle that ill-gotten righteousness is the ultimate poison rest at the foundation of Alcoholics Anonymous. Anyone who has found sobriety in AA faces one colossal roadblock to dismissing what has been alleged in this book about long-term sobriety and works righteousness.

Chapter 14

The Greatest Genus Of Alcoholics Anonymous

*T*he anonymity feature of AA, and a close derivative of it, must leave AA old timers and churchgoers convinced that "works righteousness" is the dominate, deadly poison of spiritual growth. AA's success is a direct result of the program's method of dealing so effectively with the nastiest flavor of this deadly poison. AA has recognized works righteousness in the form of reputation-building as the ultimate poison from the very beginning. Anonymity is paramount in AA and the acknowledged spiritual foundation of the program. Anonymity is the fingerprints of God on the AA design. AA would have <u>no</u> success treating addiction if the Steps of recovery did not rest on anonymity's two pillars of Biblical bedrock.

Pillar One

Telling someone "I don't care what anybody thinks about me" is a ridiculous statement. If you don't care what I think, why are you telling me you don't care what I think. No single proclamation can reveal a lack of self-awareness quite like that one. The most harden criminal fears "the hole's" solitary confinement for there is no approval to be sucked, no reputation to build, in isolation.

Being able to influence other's evaluation of our "insides" is the power of our "outsides." It's a mighty power. Witness the advent of social media. Over a billion people have a Facebook account. Electronic reputation crafting has proven to be quite the intoxicant for many. The need to influence other's view of us, the worship of our reputations, is the shared, debilitating addiction of mankind. Posing to win the esteem of our fellows hobbles those who want to live free of the works righteousness beast.

 A chronic alcoholic has very little wherewithal to influence another's perception. One way to characterize the downward spiral of addiction is a loss of such influence. The upward spiral of recovery can be characterized as regaining the power to influence other's estimation of our worth. It is not hard to see how the recovering alcoholic can fall prey to worshiping a restored reputation. Restored reputations can be lucrative. The world's stamp of approval feels really good too. The problem is that the unbelieving masses can't avoid giving credit to the recovered alcoholic for manufacturing sobriety. Getting credit for God's handiwork has proven to be spiritual suicide when it comes to alcoholics.

 AA must be "anonymous" to protect the fellowship and its members from this horrid reality. Anonymity is AA's most distinguishing genus. Because restored reputations happen so frequently in AA, the fellowship understands the work righteousness associated with reputation intimately.

Most people outside AA think the fellowship is anonymous because of the newcomer's embarrassment at being discovered to be a weak-willed alcoholic. It is true those who have suffered loss after loss, embarrassing episode after embarrassing episode, slide in the door of AA hoping to be unseen. Getting help for their dilemma is top secret. The world's harbored prejudice and misunderstanding about addiction holds power to the very end. Even a chronic alcoholic yields to the ancient curse of Adam by pridefully desiring to salvage whatever scraps of a "good" reputation that remain. "I hope no one finds out I lack the will power to fix myself. God has sentenced me to AA. God hates me!" You can't help but chuckle at such a stupendous misread but it's entirely understandable.

Fear not, for the vast majority of those who start to recover in AA get over the "AA embarrassment" quickly. The pink cloud of sobriety many times propels these spiritual embryos into evangelist fervor or just plain self-glorification. "Look everybody I'm sober!" Or "look family I'm sober." The clueless get on the loose. They have no idea that they have no idea about what's going on. Admittedly it's fun to watch. It took them a lifetime to achieve their level of sickness yet they "feel the cure" and have the answers after six months.

AA is anonymous to keep everyone in check, especially these "six-month wonders" who want to tell the world how the world works. **They fail to respect the**

monster of works righteousness that comes with getting credit for God's grace. Christians who "get religion" often behave the same way but for the sobered alcoholic the phenomenon is a deadly force of nature, or the ego as it were. AA pink clouds can be really pink.

The anonymity mandate of AA cuts works righteousness for being sober off at the knees. Displays, publicly or privately, of law-keeping righteousness are not permitted in AA, theoretically. AA has a unique and profound respect for the egotism surrounding the "reputation" problem. **The AA fellowship and the AA methodology are steeped in the practice of deflating egos.**

Anonymity's protection of the newcomer from embarrassment is an auxiliary benefit. The real shield of anonymity is to protect the fellowship from the recovering alcoholic's work righteousness and the recovering person from his ego. AA gets the magnitude of the "reputation righteousness" deception and pays homage to it's ability to squash spiritual growth in the very name of the fellowship. This top-shelf spiritual discernment deserves admiration from the Church and the medical community.

Of course, there is nothing wrong with wanting to have a good reputation, striving for a good reputation or protecting your reputation. The problem arises when our perceived reputation, what we think others think of us, starts to define us spiritually. And it is a spiritual thing because reputation touches every part of our existence.

The influence of reputation in our thought-life is unavoidable and profound. When a desired reputation and the accommodations of life that come with it start to feel like the source of our blessings, or makes us feel deserving of our blessings, humility evaporates.

Some will be able to see works righteousness in the trap of ego for what it is, some won't. It's a discernment. The issue is by no means confined to AA. In fact, the old timer in AA, knowing and understanding the AA program's emphasis on anonymity, is far ahead of most churchgoers in understanding the "reputation" trap. Crusty old AA curmudgeons know some stuff about reputation worship and what to do about it the Church would do well to emulate.

Pillar Two

Pillar two is the clearest demonstration that elimination of works righteousness is an indispensable ingredient for AA success. It is the "smoking gun" evidence that righteousness by faith (avoidance of works righteousness) is AA's secret for success. No one with any exposure to AA can doubt how directly Pillar Two addresses works righteousness. While it is easy to explain, believing it to the point of acting on it is not so easy. Internalizing the paradox of Pillar Two is a toughie.

I suppose you're like me. Fear makes me think about myself. I don't need much encouragement. I'm an easy mark. I love to think about me. I am my favorite subject. If you're like me this reality, this "bondage of self," stands between us and living life depending on God. It takes faith to move our thinking from "us" to "them" in order to help ourselves. When we think of others first we benefit the most. It's a paradox spectacularly proved and illustrated by AA's sea of sobriety.

Venturing into this paradox is not the first solution we think of when it comes to emotional pain relief. Faith born of desperation is required for the alcoholic to act so counterintuitively. The concept is void of logic outside an understanding of villainous works righteousness. Only direct evidence of the paradox has served to convince those recovering in Alcoholics Anonymous. They try it on faith. It is a big part of acting one's self into right thinking.

AA has an "in your face" methodology of forcing investigation of the paradoxical truth that we humans flourish spiritually only when we put others before ourselves. AA makes no bones about service to others being a self-serving means to a self-serving end. An alcoholic partakes of sobriety in AA through the selfish act of unselfishly helping another alcoholic. **Here is the awesome key to understanding Pillar Two- being honest about selfish motives in helping others eliminates the works righteousness that would otherwise come from putting others before ourselves. When another alcoholic uses another alcoholic to stay sober no reward for being "good" is due.**

Selfishly helping another makes works righteousness impossible. It doesn't build your reputation as a "good" person to help another for your own benefit. Those outside the AA program have an extremely hard time recognizing AA's selfishness to be selfless. Without anonymity this selflessness would never work. Earned righteousness would be unavoidable.

No member of AA will deny that one alcoholic working with another alcoholic is the most important foundation in the program of Alcoholics Anonymous. I would fairly speculate very few know the Bible attributes the effectiveness of AA relationships to designed exclusion of works righteousness. The AA program of recovery is again proven to be genus constructs of Biblical principles.

Bill Wilson and every AA sponsor in his wake has proven "selfishly" being "unselfish" is orchestrated to provide action that does not generate a works righteousness result. The lesson is beyond compelling evidence that acting one's way into right thinking instead of thinking his way into right acting, is only possible when works righteousness is not the reward. It is also compelling evidence that honesty about motives is an imperative element of the AA methodology. Seeking honesty regarding motives is a principle referenced in Step 12.

Any AA old timer will tell you right quick the task of working with newcomers is self-serving. It's how the recovered alcoholic stays anyway fulfilled in sobriety. When Bill Wilson stood in the lobby of that Akron hotel with barroom chatter rising from just down the hall there were no 12 Steps, just other suffering alcoholics. "Getting out of himself" saved Bill's backside. Bill Wilson's insight that he could stay sober working with other alcoholics sparked the formation of Alcoholics Anonymous. It was nothing else. In light of Biblical righteousness by faith doctrine it is completely understandable why Bill Wilson's insight has been so effective over the last 85 years. Rarely is the truth of any Biblical paradox so clearly in evidence.

Because there is no works righteousness in the AA model of one alcoholic helping another and because the disease concept removes one from being under the law, the 12 Steps work to spiritually awaken the alcoholic desperate enough to undertake the AA program of recovery.

Chapter 15

A Charming Couple

*A*A newcomers build faith attending meetings, reading the book and, most importantly, going through the Steps with a "sponsor." When those who have taken the 12 Steps help others do the same AA magic happens. The long-term sobriety of a recovered alcoholic is contingent on remaining spiritually fit. Spiritual conditions are maintained by working with other alcoholics as the twelfth step suggest. Men work with men and women with women.

Working with another suffering alcoholic is referred to as "Sponsoring." Sponsoring someone in AA is a privilege, despite the many headaches. AA mandates the action of love. This "AA love" has proven to be responsible for the fellowship's effectiveness and its proliferation.

A sponsor extending the hand of AA to an alcoholic can only do so from the spiritual high ground of "let me help you Grasshopper" when the teacher has something "Grasshopper" wants. The alcoholic to alcoholic interaction is the only one known to carry the relational moxie to predictably transcend the rebellion fasten so tightly in the constitution of a practicing alcoholic. Sharing the unique pain of substance abuse and being honest about motives are the distinguishing features, the juice, of these inspired collaborations.

"Grasshopper" must see the "before and after" to be anyway convinced.

A practicing alcoholic and a newly sober alcoholic are especially skeptical creatures. They project themselves and their nefarious motives onto everyone and everything else. Alcoholics wanting to get sober have manipulated people their whole life to achieve their ends. That's every alcoholic's MO and the good sponsor knows it. The AA sponsor is a different breed of cat. It takes one to know one in the case of an alcoholic.

All newly recovering alcoholics are fairly predictable. Every alcoholic that comes to AA is unable to see the truth of their motives; there is no exception. Good sponsors come well-equipped to deal with this reality. The good AA sponsor is not caught off guard. Refusing to be manipulated by these expert manipulators, the good AA sponsor doesn't just move the ball, he changes the playing field. The alcoholic knows how to play the game of self-deception by justifying feelings, rationalizing decisions and wallowing in self-pity. Good AA sponsors don't play in that ballpark. They depend on AA's "attraction rather than promotion" tradition. It's an attitude only accessible to those being selfishly unselfish.

"Pigeons," as sponsees are fondly called in AA, screw up. There is no exception to this survey either. Life newly sober has no shortage of pitfalls and the alcoholic's inability to discern motives doesn't make for the best follower of "suggestions." Non drinking screw ups come in vast varieties. Life happens. The newly sober have no concept of what it means to live life on life's terms. How could they? "Acceptance" is a foreign object.

The newly sober do all sorts of crazy things. They get married. They get divorced. They get a new job, take up a new hobby, start a business, grow their hair, cut their hair, on and on. The standard "suggestion" is to make no major decisions in the first year of sobriety. This edict makes perfect sense to the AA newcomer until it comes to them. When some shiny bait appears, like a new romantic relationship, the ease with which an AA newcomer will draw the conclusion "I'm different" is hilarious.

What separates the AA sponsor from the other folks who would like to help is the reaction of the AA sponsor to a screw up. The difference in response is critically important. Missteps in early sobriety are opportunities. The one giant gift AA can share with the Church is its approach to screw ups.

The AA sponsor doesn't take the screw up personally therefore he can't be manipulated. Family, friends and the clergy, even therapist, seem to take screw ups personally. They can't help but be "disappointed" and telegraph their message of disappointment. They are disappointed because of their personal emotional investment and the expectations that develop. However small, they have a "righteousness" investment. They get "let down" failing to understand an expectation is a premeditated resentment. At screw up time, the vast majority of the religiously disappointed also feel the need, or have the inter compulsion, to add mention of God's disappointment, just in case the offender doesn't know. **The good AA sponsor knows he can't produce surrender in the pigeon and they avoid expectations. These are two mighty distinctions**.

The AA sponsor laughs, "I told you so," or "that's a shocker," when met with most pigeon screw ups. The AA sponsor doesn't have a "works righteousness" investment in the pigeon's sobriety and it makes all the difference. The AA pigeon is not going to "let the AA sponsor down." The AA sponsor's selfish selflessness is not predicated on outcomes.

Every newcomer marvels at the amount of laughter in the rooms of AA, laughter that is completely unexpected. Churchgoers find appalling the "tragic" stories that erupt into belly laughs. "How could they be laughing at these tragedies that have stolen so much from their lives?" The copious laughter in AA is a mystery only understood by those in AA. I don't think an earth person could ever fully understand it.

Alcoholism becomes the recovering alcoholic's greatest asset. Personally, being an alcoholic is the best thing that has happened in my life. "Earth people" will never see past the tragedy of addiction to the blessing that it can be. "Good people" view such statements as platitudes or hyperbole'. The phenomenon of so much laughter in AA and what becomes funny is just hard to

A Charming Couple

explain to someone who has not made the passage. A similar psychic change is an odd thing to share.

Pigeons revealed by a screw up get irritated beyond irritation at being found predictable. They're all different remember. Forced into the classroom of an impossible-to-manipulate, know-it-all sponsor, they find themselves in a new place of powerlessness. The sponsor's altruistic motives furnish no leverage to evoke pity and no manipulating darts of alleging improper motives to throw back. Forced to accept certain things about themselves or get drunk, the busted pigeon indeed finds himself on a new playing field.

Good sponsors are, to a very large extent, in the beginning agnostic to the sponsee's willingness to follow instruction outside taking the Steps. Pigeons are surprised at how a good sponsor reacts to their failure to follow suggestions. It's a new reaction. The good sponsor has only one dog in the fight- to stay sober themselves. That's a good thing. The relationship is not contingent on the pigeon following suggestions. It's contingent on the process of getting honest. Screw ups will not get a pigeon fired but a pattern of dishonesty will.

AA screw ups are addressed from the standpoint of: "The mule is in the ditch. How do we get it out?" Focus is on how to make wrongs right. Apologies mean little. It's a Step 10 thing entirely. What does, "I'm sorry," mean anyway?

A pigeon is going to do what a pigeon is going to do. They will never be shamed into sobriety. They will never be guilted into sobriety. They will only be humbled into sobriety. The Bible says there is no condemnation for those who are in Christ Jesus. As mentioned, AA understands the value of leaving the condemnation out. Condemnation for admitted sin is never beneficial. Laying a guilt trip on the offender or cleverly shaming someone just makes matters worse. At screw up time shame and guilt are not in short supply.

In AA, words preached go in one ear and out the other. Only relating experience counts toward credibility. Effective sponsors become sacrificially transparent with those they might help to a new life. Such transparency is the opposite of reputation worship. Taking the lessons of this book we can see how both sponsor and sponsee are edified.

The Church, with its "accountability partners," or the like, don't get it. "Accountability partners" are conduct police. These relationships do not facilitate healing humility. "Rules without relationship produce rebellion." Hopefully after reading this book it is clear why conduct police have no chance. Screw up and there will be no laughter down at the church. Condemnation, lecturing, cajoling, pleading, guilt trips, shaming, anger, loveless acrimony, manipulation and secrets, there is nothing to laugh about.

A Charming Couple

The Bible calls on believers to love through witnessing. Sharing embarrassing episodes is hard. Want to know if your private witness is Biblical? Ask yourself if it's hard to give. If it doesn't cost the lover it isn't love. To love someone cost. Spouting off some call to repentance behind a righteously pointed finger or prophesying eternal damnation as someone's destiny takes no love. It cost the spouter and the prophet nothing. Can you share the things you don't want to share? That's the litmus test.

Sponsors in AA love by witnessing, by testifying, by being transparent and by understanding. Love and tolerance is their code.[47] The newly sober are often disheveled. They are incredibly self-centered ego maniacs. What they think is important most of the time isn't what's important. Sponsors listen anyway. Sponsors help find jobs. They loan money when appropriate. They answer the phone at all hours of the night. They even bail pigeons out of jail when the occasion is right. They comfort spouses upon relapse. Sponsors do all kinds of stuff. The job description is so varied it can't be written.

Strangely these activities start out as duties but invariably turn into the most rewarding experience of the sponsor's life. The opportunity to love sacrificially and have a front row seat as God reconstructs a devastated life is the coolest part of AA. Nothing else comes close. It's

---

[47] Ibid, p. 84

the faith-builder of all-faith builders. Crusty ole curmudgeon sponsors experience a very, very unique gratitude when God uses their painful experiences to heal and vanquish suffering. Painful experiences don't have the same afterlife under the rug over at the church. It's too bad religious reputation worship keeps such valuable commodities out of circulation.

A good AA sponsor has no qualms with calm, tactful confrontation. They lovingly take no "bull" to put it bluntly and every AA newcomer, without exception, comes with a "load of bull." There is no hesitation in tactfully pointing out a self-deception. Pigeons get confronted when sponsors start asking hard, uncomfortable questions. Good AA sponsors inevitably disgruntle pigeons. It's just part of the dance and disgruntlement usually marks some inflection point in the newcomer's sobriety.

Every single newcomer to AA on some level is a spoiled, immature brat. Instead of maturing by working through life's problems they drank to cope. Dulling painful feelings takes away from the painful experience's ability to teach. Dulled pain doesn't get healed. It just requires more dulling. There is no other side of dulled pain. The maturity that comes with experiencing unsettled things getting settled doesn't happen. Dulled pain hangs around.

In AA this immaturity doesn't matter. Pigeons are under no obligation to take advice. Their misery is 100%

A Charming Couple

refundable. The Big Book says if you think you're not an alcoholic go try some controlled drinking. The drinking experiment is recommended. (This part of the AA methodology freaks out church people). If the "God thing" or the truth on any myriad of subjects offends the pigeon (which it always does) then so be it. If the truth runs the pigeon out of AA, the liquor will run them back in.

Real love is a willingness to say the hard things in love without being condemning. The good sponsor cares more about the sponsee's sobriety (life) than their hurt feelings. Most pigeons spend the first two years of sobriety complaining about the unreasonableness of their sponsors and the rest of their sobriety bragging about it.

It may be hard to believe but the author has screwed up once or twice. On a particularly painful occasion I received this text message from a respected AA friend before we could speak: "I love you. It's going to be alright. Keep first things first." It was healing to the extreme in the middle of the pain. I wept in Godly gratitude. I wanted to talk to him. There was no fear of the conversation. There was no fear of repenting (my stupidity was evident). There was no fear of condemnation. And there was no pity in his words. Those words accentuated the sanctifying nature of my pain. That pain has become a huge asset in the aftermath.

It seems "good people" can't resist rehashing the episode. They mentally carry humiliating episodes around in case the offender needs the humility of a reminder. It's horrible practice that has nothing to do with humility. Morbid reflection in the rehash proves detrimental. "Hash" is enough. No "rehash" needed. Own it, confess it, suffer the consequences, make amends whenever possible, then move on. This approach prevents the sin from defining a person. Wallow in past mistakes and they will define you.

The futility of responding with anger is obvious. If anger were healing we would all find ourselves in marvelous shape. To foster healing love must govern. Love, tough and otherwise, is what AA culture so effectively utilizes at screw-up time. Good AA sponsors are slow to anger and hard to surprise.

If churchgoers get nothing else out of this book, seeing AA's response to sin as how Jesus would have us react makes it worth the read. See how the AA reaction comes without the bruising wounds of misapplied pity, anger and condemnation? Healing comes so much more readily when the dependence is on God and "His hand in all this." Any condemning response that hinders confession and transparency is counter productive in so many ways.

The "letting go and letting God" of repenting is an essential ingredient in the sweet life. Nothing facilitates a healing response to sin more than confessing to a person aware of their own sin. AA sponsors prove this spiritual law over and over. Their example and knowledge is unique in the category of human wisdom, very unique.

Chapter 16
It Works, It Really Does

The life strategy advocated by Alcoholics Anonymous and Reformed theology looks lazy and unproductive. "Letting go and letting God" and "wearing the world as a loose garment," appears to be the life of Riley. Paradoxically, nothing could be further from the truth.

Granted, the life strategy of "surrendering to win" doesn't sound like a formula for success. Being spiritually enhanced by recognizing our works righteousness schemes and seeking grace doesn't sound like the path to productivity. Surrendering to win, loving thy neighbor as thy self, valuing humility, getting by giving, developing a reliance on repentance, may be the best spiritual medicine, but these propositions appear to hold little promise as a recipe for earthly success. Intuitively, works righteousness appears to produce bigger checks that clear the bank faster.

Don't misunderstand. Just because we sweat and toil doesn't mean we do it for inappropriate righteousness; on the contrary. Paradoxically, no life strategy is more productive than righteousness by faith. A thought-life soaked in righteousness by faith turns a thought-life weighed down by problems into a thought-life focused on opportunities. The two outlooks are polar opposites. A life liberated from works righteousness is a proactive force of nature. A life spent dedicated to solving one problem after another is a reactive life of frustration.

    Seizing opportunity is a lot of work, a lot of hard work, but optimism energizes. Seizing opportunity is a fun, optimistic pursuit. The energy to seize opportunity comes from a different place. Urgent problem solving drains a person. Seizing opportunity focuses us in today. It focuses us in the moment actually.

    AA and Reformed theology reveal how fixing ourselves permeates our being. We can't compartmentalize the job of fixing ourselves when we're infected with the notion. When our righteousness comes by faith we are not preoccupied with the messages coming from the world (our circumstances). President Reagan liked to say, "there is no limit to what you can accomplish if you don't care who gets the credit." President Reagan understood the disability of works righteousness.

    When God tells us who we are problems truly become opportunities. We show up without the baggage of dual agendas. A focus split between accomplishing the goal and fixing ourselves requires getting credit for the good and blame shifting the bad.

    When our results determine our worth as human beings success brings arrogance. When focus has paid off in preparedness success brings confidence. Arrogance and confidence are completely different. Arrogance comes from a seed of fear. Confidence comes from a seed of faith. We love our confident teammates and tolerate the arrogant ones until they move on.

Freedom from being defined by the world, freedom to be who God says we are, supplies opportunities for really good stuff to happen in our lives. Self-focus clogs productivity. Operating in grace takes the pressure off. Avoiding self-centeredness, not taking ourselves so seriously, we can focus on what is important.

A focused life is about the details. To become masters of any craft requires the details be mastered. Conquered details don't overwhelm us with righteousness. The right collection of conquered details are a massive cumulative success. Whipping details is the right fight.

When our righteousness comes from works righteousness we need big things. When everything that happens and all our circumstances are a commentary on our self worth life is like drinking from a fire hose. Needing big things, we don't have time to suck the small commentaries on who we are from details. When our focus is not on the details life is urgent. This is counterintuitive. Unattended details leave us unprepared. Unprepared equals urgent. Unpreparedness makes everything urgent. No one can be their most productive and overwhelmed at the same time. Being a slave to the urgent distracts us from what is important.

Clemson University Head Football Coach Dabo Swinney understands. He has built the Clemson Tiger football program into a great example of the success righteousness by faith achieves. Despite being accused of being too religious or being too "down home," Coach Swinney has disrupted the world of college football using the fundamentals explained in this book. Dabo's success has come from being Dabo. William Christopher (Dabo) Swinney is really good at hearing who God says he is. The world doesn't tell Coach Swinney who he is or needs to be. His fantastic success started right there.

  Coach Swinney has taken "little ole Clemson" to unprecedented heights in the hotly contested world of college football by focusing on the development of a culture. The focus of that culture is to serve the players' best interest. In the best traditions of an AA sponsor, Coach Swinney has built a college football juggernaut through selfish service to others. Coach Swinney's philosophy is the epitome' of servant leadership. He understands the paradox that givers get.

  Clemson's players are known for their preparedness and their ability to perform their best on the biggest stages. When the pressure is on the Tigers are at their best. Coach Swinney's culture produces players that "play loose," unafraid of failure. They are prepared. They are confident. They have been focused on, and have taken care of, the details. Taking care of the details has made the players masters of their craft.

  Football is a violent, physically demanding sport. Coach Swinney talks to his players about taking "the Eye of the Tiger" on the field. "The Eye of the Tiger" is a euphemism for exuding the confidence and aggression required to "dominate the moment." The players have confidence to play one play at a time. The Clemson culture has them in the moment. "The Eye of the Tiger" doesn't let the mistakes of the previous play beat you on the next play. "The Eye of the Tiger" is focus and endurance born in preparation. It's not an emotion ginned in pregame hype. Taking care of the details off the field brings "the Eye of the Tiger" onto the field. There is no fear, only faith, in "the Eye of the Tiger." "Wearing the world as a loose garment" plays a big part in "the Eye of the Tiger." "The Eye of the Tiger" requires righteousness by faith.

The players success or failure on the football field does not define the them as men. Coach Swinney strives to create an atmosphere that challenges each member of the team to be the best version of themselves they can be. "Best is the standard," individual best, not comparative best. He understands "comparing" puts limits on individual growth. Coach Swinney is very intentional about instilling this attitude through out Clemson's football program. His dedication to seeding this attitude throughout Clemson's program is the innovation of his culture. His success disrupted the game (industry) of college football because he executed so well on this fundamental. Coach Swinney executes a branding strategy the most accomplished corporate executive would admire. The brand is loving one another and focusing on the details.

Coach Swinney concentrates on taking boys and building men, not football players. Before Clemson's success many thought Coach Swinney's philosophy was a gamble. It was never a gamble. Parents want prepared young men not prepared football players. Coach Swinney attracts the best football talent in America for that reason. Clemson is very selective in who they recruit. Young men who are not fixing their "insides" with "football outsides" are attracted to Clemson, and vice versa. While other powerhouse college football programs send out scholarship offers to all the top players, Clemson is very, very selective with their offers.

Coach Swinney's Tigers have played for the last 5 national championships and won 2 (as of this writing). One might assume undefeated seasons and National Championships are the team's goals. This isn't so. Coach Swinney refuses to measure his teams by their won/loss record. The team enjoys each success and learns from each setback. Coach Swinney was the first coach to emphasize the importance of the program's culture over every other consideration.

Coach Swinney convinced an administration focused on revenue to change their focus to the players. The best players are attracted by a player-centric culture that provides teenagers with what they need not necessarily what they want. Again, the approach was counterintuitive. Dabo runs a tight ship. He convinced the administration that his culture would attract the best players and the revenue would follow the best players. He was not-so-incredibly prophetic. The result has been a win/win of historic proportion. The players win. Clemson wins. The fans win. The football staff wins. The state of South Carolina wins. Coach Swinney wins. A culture focused on the details wins. Cultures focused on winning have proven unable to compete with Clemson.

Clemson leads the nation in percentage of players graduated year in, year out. The academic support team at Vickery Hall is the envy of the nation. Clemson competes with Duke and Northwestern for the highest academic achievement ranking year in, year out. Clemson plays more players per game than any other team. Coach Swinney is dedicated to having his players play football while they get an education, not get an education while they play football. "Paw Journey" is a program that allows players to intern on a short-term basis with corporate America or travel the world to preform acts of service to the underserved. Clemson football is a cultural program, not a football program. It's a righteousness by faith program.

Clemson's football culture rest upon a foundation of valuing gratitude and humility as portrayed in previous chapters. Coach Swinney says, "to be an over-achiever you have to be an over-believer." Dabo Swinney gets it. His career and faith are not compartmentalized. His righteousness comes from faith not works. The success of Clemson football comes from relying on paradox. Scriptural truth is at the heart of the Clemson culture. It's a great example of the truths contained in this book bringing success.

  Leading a productive life filled with gratitude is all about picking the right struggles. At Clemson the struggle is to believe. On his first day as head coach, Coach Swinney demanded his players "be all in" or go home. He offered to help anyone who wanted to transfer do so. That took guts. Most coaches would have been begging the best players to stay. From day one Coach Swinney has demanded the team come first. The strategy demanded surrender individually to win as a team. Not a single player went home or transferred.

  Another "Daboism" is, "It's not what happens to you in life but how you respond that counts." No human life dodges pain and sorrow. How we respond to life's most painful episodes will determine the fullness or emptiness of our lives. Our response to life's hardships determines whether we will be victims or "accepters." How we are affected by the pain that comes from episodes of life's trauma determines the quality of our thought-life.

  Those who can't "accept life on life's terms" fight unwinnable battles. Being unable to "accept" mires one in the lost battles of yesterday or battles of the future that need not be fought. Those who have the faith to "accept" life in the moment are irrepressible. The challenges of today are where victory or defeat is determined. Jesus talked a lot about how faith allows us to live in today.

The only challenges that matter are found in "today." It's the little things. Once you understand this principle a love for life replaces a fear of life. When our thought-life gets centered outside of "today" we flail about wasting emotional and physical energy on things we can't control. Righteousness by faith instigates the "wherewithal" to focus in "today." Works righteousness is heavy, urgent and without focus. Works righteousness is the ultimate buzz kill.

For the recovered alcoholic whose spiritual experience is limited to monolithic exposure to AA or the Christian mired in legalism there is more to God's promises than you know. There is a mighty sparkle in God's kingdom, an undiscovered, indescribable freedom. A life-sail masted by faith is the most freeing thing. Only a thought-life dominated by faith that God is not Santa Claus can bring true freedom. Understanding why a loving God gave us the law to increase sin is essential to understanding the Gospel. Sitting in the lap of ole Saint Nick deservedly reciting our wish lists is a miserable, unfulfilling life. Crying over lumps of coal in self-pity is worse.

The gratitude that comes from living life trying to believe I am who God says I am is the most excellent experience. It's freedom. No masks needed. Pain does not mean loss of joy. We mourn in peace and celebrate victory in gratitude. Having a joyful, peaceful spirit rocks! Unshakable joy is the ticket to being loved and receiving love. And feeling loved for who we really are is the happy place our hearts crave above everything else.

Conclusion

*J*esus walked. He talked. He slept. He ate. He cried. He prayed, a lot.

Jesus also performed miracles. With his Disciples teetering on the brink of drowning in a violent sea, Jesus walked on water. Jesus didn't run on water. He walked. Scripture depicts Jesus always at the same pace. He was never in a hurry. Jesus never ran anywhere for any reason. He didn't gallop into Jerusalem on the back of a stallion. He rode a donkey.

His contemporaries often pleaded with Jesus to hurry. He never did. Mary and Martha sent word to Jesus that Lazarus, the one he loved, was dying hoping he would come immediately. He waited two days. Jesus' faith was perfect. He knew his Father's power. Upon arrival Jesus raised Lazarus from the dead. Jesus found no need to be hastened by life nor death. Jesus' perfect reliance on the Father found him poised no matter the gravity of any circumstance. Jesus always acted proactively, never reactively.

Those under the law out to please God are in a hurry. I understand. They have much to do and not much time to do it. Believers depending on God know patience and calm. They can afford it. Jesus' perfect record is theirs. Those under the law out to please God by earning their righteousness have a life of problems to solve. Believers depending on God have a life of opportunities

Conclusion

to seize. Trusting God is a job with focus- loving, praying, worshiping and using His gifts to serve others. Trying to please God by solving life's problems is a nightmare for even the most gifted multitasker. It's a frustrating existence spent urgently swimming up stream.

Life is hard. There are attitudes and perspectives that can make life easier but never easy. The easiest way to make life easier is to stop making life harder. Humans have an ingenious knack for making life harder. The world wounds us, we retaliate. The world demands, we try to deliver. Life gets more difficult with every salvo and every demand. "Look what they make me do to myself."

Under the law, we squeeze what has been created for the stuff only the Creator can provide. Undetected, our hidden addictions bring a deepening denial of our powerlessness. Under the law our thought-life is a struggle to find ourselves to be a "good" person. Our focus is on what we want and what we need to get it. We hotly pursue what we want as though other want will not replace it immediately. Our sense of the *quid pro quo* carries over from our relationship with God to dominate our relationship with the world. We maneuver to avoid being deprived by fate or the crafty plans of others.

Works righteousness produces an ever-present, unsettling angst. The angst of works righteousness leaves us with the dissatisfaction of always having unfinished business in our lives. This dissatisfaction corrupts our thought-life. This sense of unfinished business blinds us to the truth life is a journey not a destination. Under the law rest produces guilt. Under the law we always have something to prove, to ourselves mainly.

Law-keeping righteousness is the most sinister provocateur. It outwits us constantly. We are easily fooled by the notion something outside us is required for contentment. Under the law this notion designates our ambitions. Absent faith we struggle to accomplish mission impossible. Under the law, shackled by works righteousness, we are stuck solving another flavor of the same ole unsolvable problem of "self." Our addictions, our faithless righteousness schemes, mire us in life's pain or march us on endless attempts to out flank it, or both.

Righteousness by faith breeds a life marked by courage, humble gratitude and an unshakable joy. Thusly armed, the believer walks through pain then leaves it behind. Faith our pain is not pointless or punishment builds a healthy thought-life. The faithful thought-life rest in the security that God loves us no matter what and that He will never love us more or less than He does right now. Righteousness by faith allows us to walk through pain without losing our joy. Righteousness by faith fuels optimistic lives liberated from drudgery. In the kingdom of God hope never dies.

Conclusion

The goal of this book has been to explain and demonstrate why the Biblical paradox of grace holds so much power. The sobriety in Alcoholics Anonymous has been attributed to the power of grace. Godly humility has been demonstrated to be the key to AA's success. Any disagreement must start with an alternative explanation of AA's history of sobriety.

Hopefully the reader has been amazed by gratitude's mysterious and mighty power.

Hopefully the reader is convinced an investigation of Biblical Christianity is not a journey into legalism but just the opposite.

Hopefully the reader has been shown that Alcoholics Anonymous works by channeling desperation into faith.

Hopefully the lens of Scripture has revealed AA is fundamentally "righteousness by faith" and nothing else.

Hopefully the reader has discovered the AA experience illustrates the truth of Biblical paradox as no other modern phenomenon.

Hopefully understanding God's law is a mirror has revealed how hidden addictions use works righteousness to camouflage themselves in our thought-lives and rob our freedom.

These are my hopes. God bless you all.

THE END

Appendix

The AA Promises

The Big Book promises certain things will happen in recovery after Step 9. No text survives 85 years with the credibility of the Big Book making unkept promises. These promises are read at every AA meeting. The AA experience has proved them true without caveat.

Here are "The Promises" taken from page 83 and 84 of the book, *Alcoholics Anonymous*:

"If we are painstaking about this phase of our development, we will be amazed before we are half way through. We are going to know a new freedom and a new happiness. We will not regret the past nor wish to shut the door on it. We will comprehend the word serenity and we will know peace. No matter how far down the scale we have gone, we will see how our experience can benefit others. That feeling of uselessness and self-pity will disappear. We will lose interest in selfish things and gain interest in our fellows. Self-seeking will slip away. Our whole attitude and outlook upon life will change. Fear of people and of economic insecurity will leave us. We will intuitively know how to handle situations which used to baffle us. We will suddenly realize that God is doing for us what we could not do for ourselves.

Are these extravagant promises? We think not. They are being fulfilled among us- sometimes quickly, sometimes slowly. They will always materialize if we work for them."